To Suzie

Hope you learn
enough phrases
Tibetan Phrasebook to make
it to Tibet.

Yanki

Tibetan Phrasebook

Andrew Bloomfield and Yanki Tshering

Snow Lion Publications
Ithaca, New York USA

Snow Lion Publications
P.O. Box 6483
Ithaca, New York 14851
USA

First Edition U.S.A. 1987
Second Edition U.S.A. 1991

Printed in USA

Library of Congress Catalog Number

Bloomfield, Andrew, 1960–
    Tibetan phrasebook.

    1. Tibetan language—Conversation and phrase
books—English   I. Yanki Tshering, 1957–
II. Title.
PL3613.B58   1987   495'483421   87–12989
ISBN 0-937938-54-8

Table of Contents

Acknowledgements

I am grateful to the kind staff at Snow Lion Publications—Calvin Smith, Pat Aiello, Sidney and Yvonne Segal-Piburn, Jeff and Christine Cox—for their support as well as the use of their equipment. Also, thanks to Khamlung Tenzin, who first introduced me to the Tibetan language, for his encouragement and help.

Most sincere thanks to Audrey Sheridan who, during the preparation and completion of this manuscript, showed great patience, offered valuable suggestions and displayed sheer endurance.

> Andrew Bloomfield
> Ithaca, New York

I would like to thank Sidney Piburn of Snow Lion Publications without whose enthusiasm and encouragement this project would have remained just an idea.

Special thanks are also due to Tsedan Chonjore, Kama Joshi, Paul Kaplan and my co-workers Sonam and Dawa of the Experiment in International Living in Nepal. I would also like to thank Philip Hemly for help in making the cassette tapes.

> Yanki Tshering
> New York City, New York

Two 90-minute cassette tapes are available if you would like to hear how the words and phrases are spoken by a native. They can be obtained for $12.95 plus $3.00 shipping from:

Snow Lion Publishing
P.O. Box 6483
Ithaca, NY 14851
Tel: 800-950-0313 Orders only,
     or 607-273-8519.

PART ONE

INTRODUCTORY MATERIAL

Preface

The purpose of this book and accompanying tapes is to give you the skill to converse in Tibetan in as short a time as possible. No prior foreign language skills are needed, nor a capacity for learning foreign languages. You need only become familiar with the various sounds in the phonetic system, learn the phrases you feel are most important, and listen to the tapes to make sure your pronunciation is correct. Smiles of recognition, warm invitations, and pleasant surprises will follow. It has been our experience that when westerners give an inch towards communication, Tibetans give a mile.

Introduction

We hope this book meets a growing demand by travelers these days: the desire to converse with Tibetan people. Many have voiced the same frustration, "Tibetans seem so interesting and friendly, I wish I could say just a few words to them." Though some material has been published to achieve this result, past attempts at such a book have been relatively ineffective. We feel their errors are three-fold.

Words and sentences that are introduced are either ones you wouldn't really use or ones that may be grammatically correct, but different from the way natives actually say them. The second drawback is the lack of cultural preparation. These books do not familiarize you with the customs and rituals you are sure to encounter.

The greatest problem, however, is the unintelligible way Tibetan words have been romanized. Nuances of Tibetan pronunciation that authors try to capture in English make voicing the actual word impossible. As there is no lucid standard form to rely upon, each author makes up a system to emphasize his or her idea of how the language is spoken.

The information found in this book has been compiled by both a western and a native speaker based on their experiences with Tibetan people. Some additional information has been supplied by friends who have recently returned from Tibet. Though the focus of this material is on the country of Tibet, the phrases introduced are equally as applicable to those interacting with Tibetans in Nepal, India, or anywhere else. Outside Tibet, however, certain common words are replaced by their indigenous counterparts. In Nepal, for instance, Tibetans will usually use the Hindi or Nepali words for "sugar" and "shoes." Similarly, in Tibet these days certain Chinese words are used in place of Tibetan ones.

The material presented is specific to typical situations one might encounter: going to a restaurant, traveling with pilgrims, visiting a monastery, and so on. Not only do the dialogues present cultural customs and mannerisms as you will find them, they also provide valuable tips about specific places of interest in Nepal and Tibet. They prepare you for visiting a Tibetan doctor, understanding proper etiquette in a monastery—even what to expect on a journey overland.

Regarding the romanization of Tibetan, we have gauged ours more for the English speaker to "get by" than for a precise, nativelike result. We can afford to offer this simplified way of pronunciation because dialects vary so much from province to province. Therefore slight differences of language pronunciation are common, and Tibetan ears are tolerant. Nuances of pronunciation are not necessary to perfect at the beginning level, and will make little difference in being understood.

Besides clear romanization, we feel tapes to complement this book are an indispensible item. They allow you to actually hear the written words in the book being spoken by a native. Spaces between phrases let you repeat the phrases aloud as you follow along in the book. Or, you can listen to the tapes with a headphone tape player while driving to work, jogging, washing the dishes—whenever.

If you are in a Tibetan environment, you can fast-forward the tapes to the place that corresponds to your present situation, say for instance if you are at a monastery or bazaar and want to hear those very dialogues. If you run into the problem of not being understood at all, you may want to play your host the phrase directly from the tape player.

1 Use Of This Book

An important part to this book is the phonetic system. It is the blueprint for the entire text and tapes. Memorize what each romanized vowel or consonant sounds like before going further. As will be explained shortly, hyphenated words should be spoken together quickly, as if they were one word. Otherwise space the words as you would in English.

Following the phonetic explanation is the grammar section, providing only the barest of information—enough to work with at the beginning level. To go any further into the precise modes of the language, the exceptions to the rules, or details where we have merely generalized, would only add confusion. Rather than create a long introductory grammar section, we have explained many rules and structures of the language as they appear in the dialogues. This allows you to see them in their proper context.

Under the title of each section may be a paragraph or two of explanation. Following these introductory remarks are listed common phrases and helpful words with which you may want to familiarize yourself. Many are in "fill in the blank" format which tends to be easier to assimilate. The dialogues that follow contain many of the previous phrases in context.

Sentences in the dialogues are written first in English and then Tibetan. Under the Tibetan is English again, each word corresponding roughly with the Tibetan word it lies beneath (it could not be type-set exactly). This enables you to see the grammatical schema of the Tibetan language, as well as isolate words you may want to emphasize.

If you are not being understood when using a sentence from this book, go back and take the most important words from the sentence and just say those.

Some of the dialogues are quite long. We suggest you pick those phrases you feel to be most important, and study them. The others can be referred back to should the need arise. In the back of the book is a vocabulary list. Though these words may not have been reviewed in the body of the text, explanations on the grammatical use of words have been given, so you will know how to use them.

The most important introductory remark we can impart is that you try to communicate with Tibetans. Entire afternoons have been spent conversing with just the words "good" and "not good". Tibetans love it! With the question "What is this?" you can learn huge amounts of vocabulary. Give it a try, don't be afraid to make mistakes, and enjoy!

2 Phonetic System

VOWELS

a and *ah* are the "a" sound in f*a*ther. (drog-p*a*:nomad/k*ah*-yul: cup)

ay is the "ay" sound in pl*ay*. (r*ay*:is)

e and *eh* are the "e" sound in l*e*t. (d*e*-tsi:a little/z*eh*-bo:beautiful)

i is the "e" sound in rel*i*eve. (ny*i*-ma:day)

ee is a longer "e" sound, the "ie" in rel*ie*ve. (r*ee*:mountain)

o is the "o" sound in l*o*w. (p*o*:old man)

oo is the "oo" sound in m*oo*n. (z*oo*-mah:fake)

ö is the German umlaut sound, similar to the "u" in p*u*t. (Ph*ö*:Tibet)

u is the "u" sound in sc*u*ba. (nor-b*u*:jewel)

ü is an umlaut "u", similar to the "oo" in l*oo*t. (ng*ü*:silver;money)

CONSONANTS

ky is pronounced basically like the word "key". *Kye*, then, would be pronounced like the *Kie* in "Kiev". (*kye*:take)

ng is a simple sound to pronounce and commonly used. The back of the tongue presses against the roof in the back of the mouth while you sound "ng", like the end of the word "si*ng*". Then drop the tongue down quickly to an "ah" sound. (*ng*ah-tso:we)

ny is pronounced like the "ny" in ca*ny*on. (*ny*ö:buy)

tsa is the "ts" at the end of the word gri*ts*, plus the addition of the "ah" sound. (*tsa*h-po: hot)

Helpful Hints

1) The consonant "g" is always hard. It should never be pronounced like a "j".

2) Don't be tricked into mispronouncing a word that may be spelled like an English word. *Lung* (air;wind), for instance, is not pronounced like the human organ, but with a "u" sound as in the word "sc*u*ba".

3) Words like *mo-tah* (car) and *shi-tah* (very), may be pronounced with an "r" sound in the second syllable : *mo-tra* and *shi-tra*. Others like *trahng-mo* (cold), *sar-pa* (new), and *kar-ma* (minute;star), may be pronounced without the "r" sound in the first syllable: *thang-mo*, *sah-pah*, and *kah-mah*. Don't let these differences confuse you, for pronunciation does not affect the words' meaning.

ASPIRANTS AND NONASPIRANTS

Aspiration is the forceful exhalation that accompanies a consonant. An example of aspiration and non-aspiration can be found in the word "total"—the first *t* is aspirated while the second *t* is not. The use of aspiration in Tibetan is important in differentiating one word from another. In order to distinguish between a word that needs aspiration and one that does not, we add an "h" after the particle that needs aspiration, and leave it off when aspiration is not needed.

Examples:

> unaspirated:**k**ang-ba (leg/foot)
>   aspirated:**kh**ang-ba (house)
> unaspirated:**ch**a-la (things) The *ch* is not hard, but
>   soft like the *ch* in "child".
>   aspirated:**chh**ak (break)
> unaspirated:**t**a (horse)
>   aspirated:**th**an-dah (now)
> unaspirated:**p**ah-la (father)
>   aspirated:**ph**a-mah (parents)
> unaspirated:**ts**a (grass)
>   aspirated:**tsh**a (salt)

You might be tempted to pronounce something you see written with a "th" like the "th" in "this". Or something written "ph" like an "f". Remember that the "h" that follows consonants, except for *c*, is only an aspiration marker.

3 Grammar

Tibetan is a language made up of monosyllabic parts. Many of these parts have independent meanings that, when strung together, combine to make new words. The hyphens we use to separate the words in this book show the junction of such syllables. You should not treat each as a separate word by pausing between every particle. Rather they should be spoken together quickly, with brief breaks between syllables where regular spaces exist. (Syllables are sometimes hyphenated that should not ordinarily be combined, in order to duplicate the way words are actually spoken). You should not be concerned with which of the two or three syllables to accent. The proper accent automatically occurs as a result of the phonetic system we use. For instance, the double "oo" in the second part of the word for "pants" (*khu-doong*) makes you naturally accent the second syllable—the correct pronunciation. The general flow of the language will become obvious when listening to the tape.

You may notice that two or three different words have the same spelling. For instance, the word for "head" and "door" are both spelled the same (*go*). How do you pronounce one differently from the other? You don't. The difference lies in the use of subtle tones that exist in the Tibetan language, the introduction of which is beyond the scope of this book. However, the tones are so subtle that many times even Tibetans cannot tell them apart. Thus the Tibetan saying: you can tell what word was meant only from the context in which it was used.

If you visit a Tibetan doctor and complain of a sore head (*go*), the sentence structure you use and other obvious factors will make it impossible for him to think that you are complaining of a sore door (*go*).

NOUNS

Nouns in Tibetan are singular words. Definite and indefinite articles like "a" and "the" are not used. However, demonstrative adjectives like "this/that" (*di/pha-gi*) "these/those" (*din-tso/phan-tso*) are used. To make a noun plural you add *-tso* to the noun or *n* + *-tso* to the demonstrative adjective.

chair:**koop-kyah**	—	this chair:**koop-kyah di**
chairs:**koop-kyah-tso**	—	these chairs:**koop-kyah din-tso**
book:**teb**	—	that book:**teb pha-gi**
books:**teb-tso**	—	those books:**teb phan-tso**

Other Helpful Words

that,up there: **yah-gi**	those,up there:**yahn-tso**
that,down there:**mah-gi**	those,down there:**mahn-tso**

If you can't remember the correct demonstrative adjective, just use *di* (this). *Di* can be used for just about everything—"this," "that," "those" and so on—especially when the particular object you are addressing is in sight.

SENTENCE STRUCTURE

The form of Tibetan sentence structure is as follows:

1)   subject   +   object   +   verb
        Ngah   **Tom**   **yin**
        (I)   Tom   (am): I am Tom.

2)   **Di**   **koop-kyah**   **ray**
        (this)   (chair)   (is): This is a chair.

There is no article to denote *a* chair—it is implied. If you want to specify "one" of something, for instance "one chair," use the word for "one" (*chik*).

3)   One chair is there.
        Koop-kyah chik pha-ghey du
        (chair)   (one) (there)   (is)

PRONOUNS

I	**ngah**
you	**keh-rahng**
he/she	**khong**
we	**ngah-tso**
you (plural)	**keh-rahng-tso**
they	**khong-tso**

Accusative

The accusative case shows you who or what received an action:

                    He gave it *to me*.

subject	+	instrumental (*gi*)	+	accusative	+	verb
Khong		**gi**		***ngah la***		**teh-song**
(he)		("instrumental")		(to me)		(gave)

me	**ngah la**
you	**keh-rahng la**
him/her	**khong la**
us	**ngah-tso la**
you (plural)	**keh-rahng-tso la**
them	**khong-tso la**

Possessive

The possessive case shows ownership:

                    This is *yours*.

subject	+	possessive	+	verb
Di		***keh-rahng gi***		**ray**
(this)		(yours)		(is)

my	**ngey** (formed by ngah + gi)
your	**keh-rahng gi**
his/her	**khong gi**
our	**ngah-tsö** (or) **ngah-tso gi**
your	**keh-rahng-tsö** (or)
	keh-rahng-tso gi
their	**khong-tsö** (or) **khong-tso gi**

The shortened possessive form shown above: **ngah** + **gi** becoming **ngey**, is found in other instances as well:

"Tibetan food" changes from **Phö-ba gi kah-lah** to **Phö-beh kah-lah**.

"monastery's incense" changes from **gom-pa gi pö** to **gom-peh pö**.

The possessive **gi** can be used in other ways:

4) the price of the fruit
   shing-do gi kong
   (fruit)   (of) (price)
5) the lama's throne
   la-ma gi shug-ti
   (lama)(of)(throne)

VERB CONJUGATION

The verb "to be" does not generally show tense or number. Tenses and number are denoted by other words in the sentence like pronouns, nouns, and objects. The verb "to be" may seem a bit confusing at first, for it is a difficult part of Tibetan grammar. What follows is the verb "to be" introduced in its three forms:

A) *To Identify*
   First Person:**yin** (am)   Second/Third Person:**ray** (are/is)

Examples:
   6) I am Sidney.   7) You are Audrey.
   Ngah Sidney yin   **Keh-rahng Audrey ray**

8) He is Jeff.
   Khong Jeff ray

B) *To Express Existence*
   First Person:**yö** (am)   Second/Third Person:**du** (or) **yo-ray** (are/is)

9) I am in Tibet.

   Ngah Phö la yö

   (I) (Tibet) (in)(am)

10) You are at the monastery.
    Keh-rahng gom-pa la du
    (or) **yo-ray**
    (you)   (monastery) (at)
              (are)

Why do we give the choice of using either **du** or **yo-ray** for the second and third person conjugations? Though they are both verbs of existence, **du** is used when the speaker has actually experienced what he or she is talking about. If the speaker has been to Tibet and has seen yaks there, he or she can say:

11) In Tibet there are yaks.
    Phö la   yak du
    (Tibet in) yak (are)

If the speaker has not been to Tibet, but knows there are yaks in Tibet, he or she would say:

12) In Tibet there are yaks.
    Phö la   yak yo-ray
    (Tibet in) yak (are)

Despite this difference, if you want to begin speaking the language without getting too particular, Tibetans will understand both. If you use **du** without having experienced what you are talking about, or **yo-ray** when you have, don't worry about it. When you hear others using these forms at least you will know the difference they are making.

C) *To Express Possession*
   First Person: **yö** (have)
   Second/Third Person: **du/yo-ray** (have/has)

13) I have a book.
    Ngah la teb yö
    (I)   (book)(have)

14) You have a book.
    Keh-rahng la teb du
    (you)   (book) (have)

15) He has a camera.
    Khong la pahr-che du
    (he) (camera) (has)

16) He has a camera.
    Khong la pahr-che yo-ray
    (he) (camera) (has)

The difference between using **du** and **yo-ray** in the last two examples follows the same reasoning given for sentences 11 and 12.

Other Verbs

To construct verb endings, whether they be past, present, or future, add the appropriate ending to the verb root. In their infinitive form, verbs will have a **pa** or **wa** suffix. This must be dropped before tense endings are added.

to drink: **thung-wa**
to eat: **sah-wa**
to buy: **nyo-wa**
to come: **yong-wa**

to talk: **keh-cha shey-wa**
to go: **chin-pa**
to meet: **toop-wa**
to sit: **deh-wa**

VERB CONJUGATION

Past Tense (Active)	*Negatives*
First Person: **verb + pah-yin**	**verb + meh**
Second/Third Person:	
verb + pah-ray	**verb + pah mah-ray**
(or) Second/Third Person:	
verb + song	**verb + mah-song**

Past Tense (Passive)	
All Pronouns: **verb + song**	**verb + mah-song**

Present Tense	
First Person: **verb + gi-yö**	**verb + meh**
Second/Third Person:	
verb + gi-du	**verb + min-du**

Future Tense
First Person: **verb + gi-yin**   **verb + gi-meh**
Second/Third Person:
   verb + gi-ray   **verb + gi mah-ray**

An active verb is one that refers to a direct object, as in "I boiled water". "I boiled" does not make sense without the referent "water". A passive verb is one that does not need an object to complete its meaning, as in "Water boiled".

A few examples showing verb conjugation and pronouns in use (see the following section for examples of negatives):

17) I will drink tea.
     Ngah cha thung-gi-yin (thung + gi-yin)
     (I)   (tea) (drink)(will)

18) He sat here.
     Khong dhey deh-pah-ray (deh + pah-ray)
     (he)   (here) (sit) (did)

19) We will meet at the monastery.
     Ngah-tso gom-pa la toop-gi-yin (toop + gi-yin)
     (we)   (monastery)(at)(meet)(will)

20) She is buying a house.
     Khong khang-ba (chik) nyo-gi-du (nyo +gi-du)
     (she) (house)   (one) (buying) (is)

21) You will talk to him.
     Keh-rahng khong la keh-cha shey-gi-ray (ke-cha shey
                                                  + gi-ray)
     (you)   (him) (to) (speak)   (will)

22) I'm going to go to the market.
     Ngah trom la dro-gi-yin (dro + gi-yin)
     (I) (market)(to)(go)(will)

23) He ate yak meat.
     Khong gi yak-shah seh-pah-ray (seh + pah-ray)
     (he)   (yak meat) (eat) (did)

The instrumental *gi* is used in the sentence above because the verb is active. The pronouns of past-tense active verb forms are followed by *gi*. If the pronoun were *ngah*, it would become *ngey*; *khong* becomes *khong gi*, and so on.

Also notice that the verb "eat," *sah*, changed to *seh* when made into past tense. Had the sentence been in the present or future tense, the verb would have remained *sah* plus the appropriate ending. Others verbs that are irregular in the past tense include:

24) "*to go*": changes from *dro* to *chin*.

a) I am going.
   Ngah dro-gi-yö
   (I) (go) (am)

b) I went.
   Ngah chin-pah-yin
   (I)   (went)

25) "*to come*": changes from *yong* to *lep*.

a) This letter is coming to the office.
   Yi-gi   di leh-khung la yong-gi-ray
   (letter)(this)(office) (to) (coming)

b) The letter arrived at (came to) the office.
   Yi-gi   leh-khung la lep-song
   (letter) (office) (at) (arrived)

Though other verbs change in the past tense, they do so in a less drastic manner.

NEGATIVES

Below are the negative forms of the verb "to be".

To Identify
First Person:
   I am: **yin**   I am not: **meh**

Second/Third Person:
   is: **ray**   is not: **mah-ray**

26) I am a westerner, not a Tibetan.
   Ngah In-jee   yin,   Phö-ba meh
   (I) (westerner)(am),(Tibetan)(am not)

27) He is a farmer, not a nomad.
    Khong shing-pa ray, drog-pa mah-ray
    (he) (farmer) (is), (nomad) (is not)

To Express Existence

First Person:
   To have (or) exist: **yö**   To not have (or) not to exist: **meh**

Second Person:
   To have (or) exist: **du**   To not have (or) not to exist:
                                                          min-du

Third Person:
   Has (or) exists: **du**   Has not (or) exists not: **min-du**

28) You have bread but no tea.
    Keh-rahng la pah-leh du yin-neh cha min-du
    (you)   (to) (bread)(have) (but) (tea) (don't have)

POSTPOSITIONS

In English, words like "to," "on," "at," and so on, are called prepositions and are used to create prepositional phrases such as "to the lake," "on the table," and "at the monastery." In Tibetan grammar, rather than precede the noun they address, these words follow it. For this reason they are called postpositions. The postposition *la* is the most versatile, since it can be used to mean "to," "at," and "on."

on top: gahng la

29) **Chog-tse gahng la teb du**: The book is on the table.
    (table)   (on) (book) (is)

under, beneath: woh-la

30) **Chog-tse gi woh-la koop-kyah du**: The chair is
                                          under the table.

    (table)   (below)   (chair)   (is)

near: (gi) thi-la

31) **Ngah keh-rahng gi thi-la yö**: I am near you.
    (I)   (you)   (near)(to)(am)

in, on, at: la

32) **Phö la**: in Tibet
    nahng la: at home

for: la

33) **Di keh-rahng la ray**: This is for you.
    (this) (you) (for)(is)

from: neh

34) **Ngah New York neh yin**: I'm from New York.
    (I)   ''   ''   (from)(am)

ADJECTIVES

Adjectives follow the noun except in cases where proper nouns
are used as adjectives:

35) I want hot food.
    Ngah la kah-lah tsah-po goh
    (to me) (food) (hot) (want)

36) This is Tibetan food.
    Di Phö-beh kah-lah ray
    (this)(Tibetan)(food)(is)

good: **yahk-po**   small: **choong choong**
many, a lot: **mahng-bo**   hot: **tsah-po**
less, a little: **nyoong nyoong**   cold: **trahng-mo**
big: **chen-po**

See HELPFUL OPPOSITES in the back of the book for a large
collection of such modifiers.

INTERROGATIVES

A) Questions are formed either by using a question word before
the verb, or by adding an interrogative particle. By question word
we mean the following:

> what: **kah-rey**
> who: **su**

where: **kah-bah**
how: **kahn-dre**
how (in what manner): **kahn-dre-si**
how much: **kah-tsö**
where from: **kah-neh**
why: **kah-rey che-neh**
when: **kah-dü**

If you use one of these words, you don't have to add an interrogative particle.

37) Where did this nomad go?
Drog-pa di kah-bah chin-song
(nomad)(this)(where) (went)

Though a question, the tone of the sentence does not rise at the end. The inclusion of the question word "where" is all that is needed to form the interrogative.

38) What is this?
Di   kah-rey ray
(this) (what) (is)

39) Where are you from?
Keh-rahng kah-neh yin
(you)   (from where)(are)

40) What is the price of this fruit?
Shing-do gi kong kah-tsö   ray
(fruit)   (of)(price)(how much)(is)

41) Why are you going to the market?
Keh-rahng trom la kah-rey che-neh dro-gi-yin
(you)   (market to)   (why)   (are going)

B) If this type of question word is not used, however, a particle must be added to the end of the sentence to form the interrogative. For the first person endings of *yin* and *yö*, the particle is *peh*:

42)   Are you going to Tibet?
      Keh-rahng Phö la dro-gi-yin-peh
      (you)   (Tibet to) (going) (are)

43)   Do you have tea?
      Keh-rahng la cha yö-peh
      (you)   (tea)   (have)

For the second and third person endings of *du* and *ray*: the particle *peh* is added to those sentences ending with *ray*, and the ending *geh* is added to those that end with *du*.

44) Is this a monastery?   45) Does he have money?
   Di   gom-pa   ray-peh   **Khong la ngü   du-geh**
   (this)(monastery) (is it)   (he)   (money)(has he)

For the past-tense form *song*, the question particle is *ngey*.

          46) Did he eat the food?
          Khong gi kah-lah seh-song-ngey
          (he)   (food) (eat) (did he)

Remember that *sah* changes to *seh* in the past tense.

Quicker Method
There is a shortened version of asking questions in both the future and past tenses. It is commonly used and easier to say. Repeating sentence 42 in the shortened future tense:
          Are you going to Tibet?
          Keh-rahng Phö la dro-geh
          (you)   (Tibet)(to)(will go)

Geh added to the verb root takes the place of *gi-yin-peh*.

The ordinary way of asking a past-tense question:
          a) Did you go to Tibet?
             Keh-rahng Phö la chin-pah-yin-peh
             (you)   (Tibet)(to)(go)(did)

The shortened past tense:
          b) Did you go to Tibet?
             Keh-rahng Phö la chin-peh
             (you)   (Tibet)(to) (went)

Peh added to the verb root takes the place of *pah-yin-peh*.

Answering Questions

At first, it is easier to answer questions than to ask them. Listen for the familiar ending of the verb, it will always be *yö, du, yo-ray, ray, yin,* or *song.* The most common you will probably hear and use are *ray* and *du.* The sound of these endings should be kept in the back of your mind. If anything follows them you can bet that you are being asked a question.

To answer, just repeat the verb with which you were asked:

a) Is this a monastery?   b) This is a monastery.
    Di gom-pa ray-peh   **Di gom-pa ray**

The questioneer has already constructed the sentence for you, just drop the interrogative particle and repeat the same sentence. The form must be adjusted to include the negative particle if necessary:

a)   Are there restaurants in Lhasa?
       Lhasa la sah-khang du-geh

b)   There are restaurants in Lhasa.
       Lhasa la sah-khang du
                 (or)

c)   There are no restaurants in Lhasa.
       Lhasa la sah-khang min-du

Yes or No Answers

Questions are easy to answer if just "yes" or "no" will suffice. You merely drop the question particle and repeat the same verb ending *after* the use of *la.* (This is a polite particle as will be seen shortly.) You can also repeat the sentence if you wish.

a)   Will you eat (some) food?
       Kah-lah sah-gi-yin-peh
       (food)   (eat) (will you)

b)   Yes, (I will eat food).
       La yin, (ngah kah-lah sah-gi-yin)
       (yes),   (I)   (food) (eat) (will)

a) Did you go to the market?
   Trom la chin-pah-yin-peh
   (market)(to)(went)(did you)

b) No, (I didn't go).
   La meh, (ngah chin meh)
   (no),   (I) (went)(not)

The shortened versions of the questions asked above:

Will you eat (some) food?
Kah-lah sah-geh

Did you go to the market?
Trom la chin-peh

COMMANDS

For a command one simply drops the infinitive form of the verb and adds one of a variety of endings. Each is used for a different honorific effect. The one we use most commonly is neither too low nor too high in respect: *ro-nahng*.

a) Please give it to me.
   Teh-ro-nahng
   (give) (please)

b) Please send the letter.
   Yi-gi tahng-ro-nahng
   (letter)(send)(please)

c) Please drink the tea.
   Cha thung-ro-nahng
   (tea)(drink)(please)

You can also drop the *ro* particle and leave *nahng* attached to the verb for a slightly less polite, or informal effect.

For a strong command just say the verb root without any tense ending:

give it!: **teh**   wait!: **gu**
look!: **tah**   come here!: **sho**
stop!: **kahk**   go away!: **gyu**
don't do that!: **mah che**   barter!: **jeh**

If someone is trying to sell you something and you appear disinterested, they may say to you: "jeh!" "jeh!". This means that you should name a price or make an offer.

SYLLABLE COMBINING

As mentioned earlier, Tibetan words are created by combining syllables. If each syllable has an independent meaning, then the combination of those create a new concept. A place of residence (*deh-sah*) is made by combining *deh*, meaning "sit" and *sah*, meaning "place". The word for "place of meditation" (*gom-gyahp sah*) is similar: "meditate" (*gom-gyahp*) plus "place" (*sah*).

Another example uses the word for house: *khang-ba*. Adding the word for medicine (*men*) to "house" creates "hospital" (*men-khang*). A tea stall is *cha-khang* (tea + house). A bedroom is *nye-khang* (sleep + house).

Some words are made by severing parts of two separate words and joining the two ends together. "Size" (*che-choong*), for example, is a combination of "big" (*chen-po*) and "small" (*choong choong*). "Houseowner" (*khang-dahk*) is a combination of "house" (*khang-ba*) and "owner" (*dahk-po*).

Several verbs are made by combining the endings -*gyahp*, -*tahng*, and -*che*, to nouns. The noun "work" (*leh-gah*) becomes the verb when -*che* is added (*leh-gah che*). A "letter" (*yi-gi*) becomes the verb "send a letter" when -*tahng* is added (*yi-gi tahng*). If you can't remember a particular verb, but know the noun you want made into a verb, try tagging on one of the above three endings.

NOTE

The most common word spoken by Tibetans is one that has many meanings. It can mean "okay," "I see," "please go on (telling your story)," and so on. Some pronounce it *lah-so*, others *les*, *les-seh*, or *lo-los*. You will come to recognize this word when others use it, and can use it yourself, especially when someone is telling you a story you've long lost the meaning of, but you want them to continue speaking! Every so often just say *lah-so*.

You may also hear the word *in-jee* or *chi-gyeh* used often. They both mean "foreigner" and can be applied to many nouns in order to denote the western equivalent. For a western restaurant, you place *in-jee* before the word for "restaurant". For the western month (Tibetans follow the lunar calendar, see DATES AND TIME) add *in-jee* to the word for "month". Western dollars are created by adding *in-jee* to the word for "coin," and so on. You will find examples of these words in the dialogues that follow.

SPECIAL STRUCTURES

Four useful structures to become familiar with are "to need," "to want," "to be allowed," and "is it alright to do."

"Desire" can be expressed a number of ways in Tibetan. Two forms are "to need" and "to want—with the intention of getting".

1) "to need" is formed by adding the suffix -*goh* to what is desired.

> I need a car.
> **Ngah la mo-tah chik goh**
> (I)   (auto) (one)(need)

-*goh* can be added to verbs as well. The following sentence ends in *yö* to signify the need for an action:

> I need to go to the market.
> **Ngah trom la dro-goh-yö**
> (I) (market)(to)(go)(need)

-*goh* can also function as a verb. Appropriate tense endings can simply be added to -*goh*:

> He will need a jacket.
> **Khong la tu-doong chik goh-gi-ray**
> (he)   (jacket)   (one)(need)(will)

Negatives can also be expressed:

> I don't need it.
> **Di mah-goh**
> (this)(don't)(need)

2) "to want—with the intention of getting" is formed by adding *dö* to the verb. In the process, the verb takes on an "n" sound.

> I want to go to Lhasa.
> **Ngah Lhasa la dron-dö-yö**
> (I)   (Lhasa)(to)(go)(want)

The meaning is that you want and plan to go to Lhasa.

The construction is: verb + *n* + *dö* (*dro* + *n* + *dö*).
Negatives are expressed by changing *yö* to *meh*:

> I don't want to eat meat.
> **Ngah shah sahn-dö-meh**
> (I)   (meat) (eat)(want)(not)

Again, the construction is: verb + *n* + *dö* (*sah* + *n* + *dö*).

3) "to be allowed": formed by adding *-cho-gi-ray* to the verb root of a sentence. This suffix tends to be spoken quickly together.

> Am I allowed to go there?
> **Ngah pha-ghey dro cho-gi-ray-peh**
> (I)   (there)   (go) (is it allowed)

The response would be:

> "You are allowed" or "You are not allowed"
> **Cho-gi-ray**   **Cho-gi-mah-ray**

4) "is it alright to do": formed by adding *nah* + *di-gi-ray-peh* to the verb. This is a conditional tense meaning "if I do something, will it be alright?" There is a slight pause after the *nah* particle and then the *di-gi-ray-peh* phrase is spoken quickly together.

> Is it okay to buy this?
> **Ngey di nyö-nah di-gi-ray-peh**
> (I) (this) (buy)(if) (is it alright)

> Is it alright to stay here?
> **Ngey dhey deh-nah di-gi-ray-peh**
> (I)   (here) (stay)(if) (is it alright)

RESPECT

Among Tibetans, adding the suffix *la* to the name of the person connotes respect. The suffix follows not only personal names but titles of address. "Father" (*pah*), for instance, becomes *pah la*. Others include:

> father: **pah la**

mother:	**ah-ma la**
older brother:	**cho la**
older sister:	**ah-cha la**
grandfather:	**po la**
grandmother:	**mo la**
monk/mister:	**ku-sho la**

These do not need the *la* suffix:

boy:	**phu**
girl:	**phu-mo**
relative:	**pin-gyah**

When trying to get someone's attention, say in a tea-stall or at the bazaar, you can call out to male persons with "older brother" or "boy," depending on whether they are older or younger than you. For females you use "older sister" or "girl" in the same way.

HONORIFICS

There is an honorific system in Tibetan that affects all significant parts of the sentence, including nouns and verbs. It makes up an entirely new list of vocabulary. Rather than teach you more than one word for a certain thing, we will just let you know that such a system exists. If, for instance, someone is asking your name and uses the word *tsen* instead of *ming* (the word we teach for "name"), they are using an honorific term. They will immediately rephrase their question with the common form of the word when they see that you do not understand.

Should you begin to use such forms, remember that they are used only when speaking of someone else. *Tsen*, for instance, is used when speaking of a person other than yourself. You always refer to your own name with the word *ming*.

4 Greetings

The following are common phrases used daily among Tibetans. Honorifics are found in phrases of greeting more than anywhere else. Don't worry if you can't immediately catch on to their use—since they are common, you'll have many opportunities to practice.

—Hello.
  Tah-shi de-leh

—How are you?
  Keh-rahng ku-su de-bo yin-peh
  (you)   (body) (well) (is it)

—I'm fine.
  La yin. Ngah sug-po de-bo yin
  (yes)   (I)   (body) (well) (is)

Note the honorific word for "body" (*ku-su*). The non-honorific form is used when speaking about oneself, thus *ku-su* changes to *sug-po* in the sentence "I'm fine".

—Please sit down.
  Shoo-ro-nahng (*shoo* is the honorific form of *deh*: sit)
  (sit) (please)

Another way of greeting is simply to ask someone where they are going:

—Where are you going?
Keh-rahng kah-bah phe-geh
(you)   (where) (are going)

Phe is the honorific form of the verb "go" (*dro*). The use of *phe-geh* is the shortened version of the question form as mentioned in the grammar section.

—Goodbye.
Kah-leh phe   (said to the person leaving, or in the
(carefully)(go)   case that both of you are leaving)

—Goodbye.
Kah-leh shoo   (said to the person remaining behind)
(carefully)(stay)

—See you later.
Jeh yong
(meet)(come)

—See you tonight.
To-gong jeh yong
(tonight)(meet)(come)

—See you tomorrow.
Sahng-nyi jeh yong
(tomorrow)(meet)(come)

—Goodnight.
Sim-jah nahng-go

Phrases like "I'm sorry" (*gong-dah*), and "thank you" (*thu-chi che*), are not commonly spoken. They should not be used as freely as they are here in the West. Only in extreme situations.

5 Useful Words in Context

1) a,an: **chik**
   >Bring *a* pen.
   >**Nyu-gu *chik* kye yong-ro-nahng**
   >(pen)   (one)(carry)(come)(please)

2) a little bit: **de-tsi**
   >Pour *a little.*
   >***De-tsi* lu-ro-nahng**
   >(a little)(pour)(please)

3) about: (gi) **kor-la**
   >He talked *about* this.
   >**Khong di gi-*kor-la* lahp-song**
   >(he) (this) (about) (talked)

4) also: **yeh**
   >I'm *also* going.
   >**Ngah *yeh* dro-gi-yin**
   >(I)   (also) (will go)

5) always: **tahk-ba-resh**
   >She *always* eats a lot.
   >**Khong gi *tahk-ba-resh* kah-lah mahng-bo sah-gi-ray**
   >(she)   (always)   (food)   (much)   (eats)

6) and: **thang**

  This dog *and* cat...
  Kyi *thang* shi-mee di...
  (dog)(and) (cat) (this)

7) both: **nyi-kah**

  I'll buy *both*.
  Ngah *nyi-kah* nyo-gi-yin
  (I) (both) (buy)(will)

8) but: **yin-neh**

  I went *but* you were not there.
  Ngah chin-pah-yin *yin-neh* keh-rahng pha-ghey min-du
  (I) (went) (but) (you) (there) (not)

9) every; each: **ray ray**

  Take one pill *every* hour.
  Chu-tsö *ray-ray* la ri-pu chik sah
  (hour) (every) (at)(pill) (one)(eat)

10) a few: **kah-shey**

  There are a *few*.
  ***Kah-shey* du**
  (a few) (are)

11) may: **chik che-nah**

  I *may* come.
  Ngah *chik che-nah* yong-gi-yin
  (I) (may) (come)

12) may not: **chik che-nah** + negative verb particle

  I *may not* come.
  Ngah *chik che-nah* yong gi-*meh*
  (I) (may) (come) (not)

13) probably: **yin-ba-drah**

  This item is *probably* an antique.
  Cha-la di nying-ba *yin-ba-drah*
  (item)(this) (old) (probably)

14) probably not: **meh-ba-drah**

> This item is *probably not* an antique.
> **Cha-la di nying-ba *meh-ba-drah***
> (item)(this) (old)   (probably not)

15) very: **shi-tah**

> It's *very* hot out now.
> **Than-dah tsah-po *shi-tah* du**
> (now)   (hot)   (very) (is)

The second syllable should be stressed in the word *shi-tah*. You will hear it this way on the tape.

Often Tibetans use the particle *peh* before that which is to be modified. This has the same meaning as *shi-tah*. Example: *than-dah peh tsah-po du* has the same meaning as sentence 15 above.

6 *Useful Phrases/ Miscellaneous Phrases*

USEFUL PHRASES

1) Do you know (speak) English?
   In-jee-keh shing-gi-yö-peh
   (English) (know) (do you)

2) Does someone here know (speak) English?
   Dhey In-jee-keh shing-ken yo-ray-peh
   (here)(English) (knower) (is there)

3) I don't eat meat.
   Ngah shah sah-gi-meh
   (I)   (meat)(eat) (not)

4) I know / I don't know.
   Ngah shing-gi-yö / Ngah shing-gi-meh
   (I)   (know) (do) / (I) (know) (not)

5) I lost my passport.
   Ngey lah-kyer lah-song
   (I) (passport) (lost)

The word *lah-kyer* can be used for any form of identification or permit.

6) I speak only a little Tibetan.
   Ngah Phö-keh de-tsi shing-gi-yö
   (I)   (Tibetan)(a little) (know)

7) I understand / I don't understand.
   Ha-kho-song / Ha-kho-mah-song

   Do you understand?: **Ha-kho song-ngey**

8) I'm hungry.
   Ngah tro-go thö-gi-du
   (I)   (hunger) (have)

9) I'm not sure.
   Ngah ten-den meh

10) I'm thirsty.
    Ngah kha-kom-gi-du
    (I)   (thirst) (have)

11) Is this water boiled?
    Chu   di   khö-song-ngey
    (water)(this)(boiled)(has been)

12) Please help me.
    Ngah la rog-pa che-nahng
    (me) (to)(help) (please)

13) Please repeat.
    Yahng-kyer soong-ro-nahng
    (again)   (say)   (please)

14) Please show me.
    Ngah la teh-nahng
    (me) (to)(show)(please)

15) Please speak slowly.
    Kah-leh la soong-ro-nahng
    (slowly)   (say) (please)

16) Please repeat slowly.
    Kah-leh yahng-kyer soong-ro-nahng
    (slowly) (again)   (say) (please)

17) Please write it down here.
    Dhey   thi-ro-nahng
    (here)(write)(please)

18) What is this?
    Di kah-rey ray
    (this)(what)(is)

19) Where is a hotel?
    Dhön-khang kah-bah yo-ray
    (hotel)   (where)   (is)

20) What is this called?
    Di la kah-rey sah
    (this) (what) (called)

MISCELLANEOUS PHRASES

1) Don't do it like that.
   Den-treh mah-che
   (like that)(don't)(do)

2) How strange.
   Ken-tsa-bo (or) Ken-tsa

3) I have forgotten.
   Ngey jeh-song (or) **Ngey jeh-shah**
   (I)   (forget)(did)

4) I know him/her.
   Ngey khong ngo shing-gi-yö
   (I) (him/her) (know) (do)

   I don't know him/her.
   Ngey khong ngo shing-gi-meh
   (I) (him/her) (know) (not)

5) Is it really?
   Ngu-ney

6) Is this enough?
   Dik song-ngey

   It is enough.
   Dik song

It is not enough.
Dik mah-song

7) It is important.
Keh-chen-po ray

It is not important.
Keh-chen-po mah-ray

8) Please say it in Tibetan.
Phö-keh la soong-ro-nahng
(Tibetan)(in)(say) (please)

9) What time is it?
Chu-tsö kah-tsö ray
(hour)   (how much)(is)

10) Where is a restaurant?
Sah-khang chik kah-bah yo-ray
(restaurant)(one)(where)(is)

11) It doesn't matter.
Keh-che-gi-mah-ray

7 Fill-In Phrases For Basic Conversation

1)   I feel _____.   **Ngah** _____ **gi-du**
   a) tired   a) **thang-che**
   b) hot   b) **tsah-du tshi**
   c) cold   c) **kyah**
   d) angry   d) **lung lahng**
   e) sad   e) **sem kyo**
   f) scared   f) **sheh**
   g) thirsty   g) **kha-kom**
   h) hungry   h) **tro-go thö**
   i) sleepy   i) **nyi-ku**

We used *tsah-po* earlier when talking about "hot weather". The personal feeling of being hot, however, is expressed by the word *tsah-du*. Similarly if some object is cold, the word *trahng-mo* is used. If somebody feels cold the word to use is *kyah*.

2)   Are you _____?   **Keh-rahng** _____
   a) going now   a) **than-dah dro-geh**
   b) ready to go   b) **dro cho-cho yin-peh**
   c) going or stayin   c) **dro-geh, dhey-geh**
   d) sick   d) **nah gi du-geh**
   e) feeling better   e) **trahk song-ngey**

3)   Where _____?   **Kah-bah** _____
   a) are you going   a) **dro-geh**

b) did you go
c) do you want to eat

b) **chin-peh**
c) **kah-lah sah-geh**

4)   I'm going to _____.
a) the post office
b) the bank
c) a restaurant
d) meander

Ngah _____ **la dro-gi-yin**
a) **drah-khang**
b) **ngü-khang**
c) **sah-khang**
d) **chahm chahm**

5)   Where is _____?
a) your house
b) the bathroom
c) the toilet
d) the bus stop
e) the bank
f) the market
g) the post office
h) the shop

_____ **kah-bah yo-ray**
a) **keh-rahng gi khang-ba**
b) **chap-sahng**
c) **sahng-chö**
d) **lahm-khor kahk-sah**
e) **ngü-khang**
f) **trom**
g) **drah-khang**
h) **tsong-khang**

6)   Please _____ me.
a) help
b) show
c) tell

Ngah la _____ **ro-nahng**
a) **rog-pah che**
b) **teh**
c) **soong**

7)   How _____?
a) good
b) far (distance)
c) long (time)
d) many

_____ **lö**
a) **yahk-**
b) **tha ring-**
c) **ring-**
d) **mahng-**

8)   What _____?
a) do you want
b) happened
c) will happen

Kah-rey _____
a) **goh**
b) **che-song**
c) **che-gi-ray**

9) What is your name?
Keh-rahng gi ming la kah-rey yin
(you)   (of) (name) (what) (is)

You would answer:
Ngah (name) **yin**
(I)   ''   (am)

10) What work do you do?
 Keh-rahng gi leh-gah kah-rey yin
 (you) (of) (work) (what) (is)

11) Please ___ with me. **Ngah nyem-do _____**
  ro-nahng

 a) have tea with me a) **cha thung-**
 b) come b) **yong-**
 c) eat food c) **kah-lah shey-** (honorific)

12) When did you come to Tibet?
 Keh-rahng Phö la kah-dü yong-pah-yin
 (you) (Tibet)(to)(when)(come) (did)

13) Two weeks ago.
 Dün-tha nyi chin-song
 (week) (two) (went)

14) How long will you stay in Tibet?
 Keh-rahng Phö la gyu-ring-lö deh-geh
 (you) (Tibet)(in)(time)(long)(how)(stay)(will)
 If *gyu-ring-lö* is not understood, try *kahp-ring-lö*.

15) I will stay in Tibet for two months.
 Ngah Phö la dah-wah nyi deh-gi-yin
 (I) (Tibet)(in)(month)(two) (stay) (will)

PART TWO

USEFUL DIALOGUES

8 A General Dialogue

—Hey boy, come here!
Phu, dhey sho!
(boy)(here)(come)

—What do you want?
Kah-rey goh
(what)(want)

—Come over here and sit down. (*a-ni* is a good word to use for
Dhey sho, a-ni dhey deh   tying ideas together)
(here)(come)(and)(here) (sit)

—How are you?
Keh-rahng ku-su de-bo yin-peh
(you)   (body) (well) (is it)

—I'm fine.
La yin (If you were not fine you would answer: *La meh*)

—What is your name?
Keh-rahng gi ming la kah-rey yin
(you)   (of) (name) (what)(is)

—My name is Pat. And yours?
Ngah Pat yin. A-ni keh-rahng
(I)   '' (am) (and) (you)

—My name is Pema.
 Ngah Peh-mah yin
 (I)   ''   (am)

—What country are you from?
 Keh-rahng loong-ba kah-neh yin?
 (you)   (country)(from where)(are)

—I'm from America/Europe.
 Ngah America/Chi-gye neh yin
 (I) (America/foreign land)(from)(am)

—That's a very nice country.
 Loong-ba pha-ghey peh kyi-bo yo-ray
 (country) (that) (very) (pleasant)(is)

—Do you have parents?   (means: Are your parents still alive?)
 Keh-rahng la pha-mah yö-peh
 (you)   (parents)   (have)

—Yes. Where are you from?
 Yö. Keh-rahng kah-neh yin
 (yes).   (you) (from where) (are)

—I'm from Eastern Tibet/Central Tibet/Northern Tibet.
 Ngah   Kham   /   Ü   /   Go-lok   neh yin
 (I) (Eastern Tibet/Central Tibet/Northern Tibet) (from)(am)

—That's far/near from here.
 Di   neh   tha   ring-bo / tha   nye-bo ray
 (here)(from)(distance) (long)/(distance) (short) (is)

—Yes. It took us two weeks to get here.
 La ray. Ngah-tsö dhey lep yah-la dün-tha nyi goh-song
 (yes)   (we)   (here)(arrive)(in order to)(week)(two)(needed)

—Where are you going now?   (note the shortened version of
 Tha keh-rahng kah-bah dro-geh   the word "now". This is a
 (now) (you)(where) (are going)   common way of using it)

—We're not sure. Have some beer.
 Ngah-tso ten-den meh. Chahng de-tsi thung/(shey)
 (we)   (sure)   (not) (beer) (a little)(drink)/(have:honorific)

—Okay, just pour a little.
Lah-so,   de-tsi   lu-ro-nahng
(okay), (a little)(pour)(please)

—Drink it all at once!
Tsahng-ma shey!
(all)   (have)

—(drinks...host pours more)
How is it?
Kahn-dre du
(how)   (is)

—It's delicious.
Shim-bu du
(delicious)(is)

—Where were you going just now?
Than-dah kah-bah chin-peh
(now)   (where)   (went)

—Near the Potala/Just around/To several monasteries.
Potala gi thi la / chahm chahm la / gom-pa kah-shey la chin-pah-yin
Potala   (near) / (meandering) / (monasteries)(several)(to) (went)

—How many brothers and sisters do you have?
Keh-rahng la pin-gyah kah-tsö yö
(you)   (to)(siblings) (how many)(have)

—I have two brothers and one sister.
Ngah la pin-gyah phu nyi thang pin-gyah phu-mo chik yö
(to me) (brothers) (two), (and) (sisters)   (one)(have)

—Are they older or younger than you?
Keh-rahng leh che-wa ray, choong-wa ray
(you)(compare)(older)(are), (younger) (are)

—One is older, two are younger.
Chik che-wa ray, nyi choong-wa ray
(one) (older) (is), (two)(younger)(are)

(choong phu: younger
brother, *choong mo:*
younger sister)

—Are you traveling alone?
Keh-rahng chik-po dro-gi-yö-peh   (*chik-po*: alone)
(you)   (alone) (going) (are)

—Yes.
La yö   (note the repetition of the form of the verb:*yö*)

—That's very strange. In Tibet we never travel alone.
Ken-tsa-bo ray. Phö la ngah-tso chik-po kah-dü-yeh dro-gi-mah-ray
(strange) (is). (Tibet)(in) (we)   (alone)   (never)
(go) (don't)

The word "never" is constructed by using *kah-dü-yeh* plus a negative particle attached to the verb.

—I like to travel alone.   (The use of *-yah* following
Ngah chik-po dro-yah gah-bo yö   *dro* is the gerund form
(I)   (alone) (going) (like) (have)   functioning like both
                                    a noun and verb)

Note the use of "to like" in the above sentence.

—Do you miss your family/homeland?
Keh-rahng gi mi-tsahng/loong-ba theng-gi-du-geh
(you)   (of) (family)/(country) (remember)

—Sometimes.
Kahp, kahp-la

—How do you like Lhasa?
Lhasa kahn-dre du
(Lhasa) (how) (is)

—I like it very much.
Ngah la Lhasa gah-bo shi-tah yö (or) **Lhasa peh kyi-bo du**
(me) (to)(Lhasa)(like)(very)(have)   " (very)(pleasant)(is)

—It is a sacred place.
Sah-cha tsa-chen-po ray
(place) (powerful) (is)

—What religion do you practice, Christian?
Keh-rahng gi chö kah-rey ray, yi-shu
(you) (of) (religion)(what)(is), (Christian)

—Yes, my family is Christian.
Ray, ngey nahng-mi yi-shu ray
(yes) (my) (family) (Christian)(is)

(nahng-mi specifies family members while mi-tsahng, used above, means "family" in general)

—No, I'm a Buddhist.
Mah-ray, Ngah nahng-pa yin
(no)   (I)   (Buddhist) (am)

—My family is Christian but I like Buddhist teachings.
Ngey nahng-mi yi-shu ray, yin-neh ngah nahng-peh chö gah-bo yö
(my) (family) (Christian)(is), (but) (I)   (Buddhist)(religion) (like)(have)

The shortened version of the possessive form *nahng-pah gi* is *nahng-peh*.

—Are you leaving?
Keh-rahng dro-geh
(you)   (going)(are)

—Yes. I have to meet my friend now.
La yin. Ngah than-dah drok-po toop-goh-yö
(yes).   (I)   (now)   (friend) (meet)(need)(have)

—Please stay a while longer.
De-tsi shoo-ro-nahng
(a little)(stay)(please)

—No, I really have to go.
La meh, ngah dro-goh-yö
(no),   (I) (go) (need)(have)

—Alright, go safely.
Di-gi-ray, kah-leh phe
(it's okay), (carefully)(go)

—Yes, stay well.
Lah-so, Kah-leh shoo
(yes),   (careful) (stay)

9 Accommodation

There are a variety of living situations available in Tibet, from expensive hotels to cheap truck stops. Some offer private rooms, others just a bed in a dorm room. Some places may not want you as a guest. If the reason you are not welcome stems from political tension, it's best to find a room elsewhere. More likely you will be turned away because they feel western standards far surpass what their humble abode can offer. In the latter case a little Tibetan goes a long way and it won't take much to convince the owners to let you stay. What better opportunity than to live in a place where Tibetan is the only spoken language! If you secure a place where no other westerners stay, it's best not to tell other foreigners about it. Your hosts probably wouldn't appreciate a bunch of westerners banging on their door for a cheap room too.

Hot water is usually brought to you in the afternoon in a thermos called a *cha-tahm*. In the case where there are four beds or so to a room, it might make sense to buy up the remaining beds in the room for privacy. In crowded conditions this may not be possible, nor would it be possible in most truck stops. In an ordinary resthouse frequented by westerners, you will probably be called upon to translate for guests once the owners find out that you know a few words of Tibetan. Also, these days it is possible to live with Tibetan families. Ask around and you may soon find yourself in the midst of a rich cultural experience.

USEFUL PHRASES

1)   I need a _____.   **Ngah la _____ goh**
  - a) room   a) **khang-mi**
  - b) bed   b) **nye-ti**
  - c) mattress   c) **bö-den**
  - d) hot water   d) **chu tsah-po**
  - e) quilt   e) **phö-kheb**
  - f) wash basin   f) **thoong-beh**
  - g) shower   g) **sug-po tru-sah**
  - h) bed linen   h) **nyeh-jeh**

2)   How much for ____?   **____ la kah-tsö ray**
  - a) overnight   a) **tsen chik**
  - b) two days   b) **nyi-ma nyi**
  - c) one week   c) **dun-tha chik**
  - d) one month   d) **dah-wah chik**

3)   Where is _____?   **_____ kah-bah yo ray**
  - a) a hotel   a) **dhön-khang**
  - b) the bathroom   b) **sahng-chö**
  - c) our room   c) **ngah-tsö khang-mi**
  - d) the shower   d) **sug-po tru-sah**
  - e) a bicycle for rent e) **kang-gah-ri la-cha la**
                                  (bicycle) (for rent)

4) Where can I put my things?
Cha-la kah-bah shah-goh-ray
(things)(where) (put) (need)

5) Please watch my things.
Ngey cha-la tah-ro-nahng
(my) (things)(look)(please)

6) What time will the hot water come?
Chu tsah-po chu-tsö kah-tsö la yong-gi-ray
(water)(hot) (time) (how much)(at)(come)(will)

7) This mattress / bed has lice / bedbugs.
Bö-den / nye-ti di la shig / bu du
(mattress)/(bed)(this)(lice)/(bugs)(has)

The word *bu* can be used for any type of bug at all. A bug bite,
is called *bu gi so-gyahp* (bug)(of)(bite).

8) May I see the room?
   Khang-mi tah cho-gi-ray-peh
   (room)   (look) (is it allowed)

9) Does sun come in the room?
   Khang-mi di la nyi-ma shah-gi-ray-peh
   (room) (this)(in) (sun) (shine) (does it)

10) Yes, this room will do/ will not do.
    Khang-mi di, di-gi-ray / di-gi-mah-ray
    (room) (this)(is alright)/(is not alright)

11) We will take all the beds in this room.
    Khang-mi di gi nye-ti tsahng-ma len-gi-yin
    (room) (this) (bed) (all) (take) (will)

12) Do you lock the front door at night?
    Tsen la goh gyahp-gi-yö-peh
    (night)(at)(door)(close)(will)

13) Do I need a key?
    Ngah la di-mi goh-ray-peh
    (to me) (key) (need)

14) I'll use my own lock and key.
    **Ngey so-sö gon-jah thang di-mi peh-chö tahng-
    gi-yin**
    (my) (own) (lock) (and) (key)   (use)
    (will)

The word *so-sö* puts emphasis on the fact that something is your
own. The verb form *peh-chö tahng* means "use".

ACCOMMODATION DIALOGUE

—Do you have a room?
   Khang-mi yö-peh
   (room) (have)(you)

—(if not) Do you know where I can find an empty room?

Khang-mi thong-ba kah-bah rah-gi-ray

(room)　　(empty)　　(where)　(obtain)(will)

—Do you know of any Tibetan families that keep western guests?

Keh-rahng gi in-jee drü-ba sha-khen Phö-beh mi-tsahng ngo

(you) (western)　(guest)　(keepers) (Tibetan) (family)(face)

shing-gi-yö-peh

(know) (do)

—(or, for a simple way): I want to stay with a Tibetan family.

Ngah Phö-beh mi-tsahng nyem-do dehn-dö-yö

(I)　(Tibetan)　(family)　(with)　　(stay)(want)

As explained above, the verb (*deh*) takes on the "n" suffix (*deh + n*) when you use the construction *dö*. The meaning of the sentence is that you want and actually plan to do something.

—How much for overnight / one week / one month?

Tsen chik / dün-tha chik / dah-wah chik la kah-tsö ray

(night)(one)/　(week)(one)　/　(month)　(one)(for)(how much)

—Westerners cannot stay here.

In-jee drü-ba　dhey　deh cho-gi-mah-ray

(western)(guests)(here)(stay)(not allowed)

—We want to stay here very much.

Ngah-tso dhey shi-tah dehn-dö-yö

(we)　　(here) (much) (stay)(want)

—Since there are no westerners here, we can practice Tibetan.

Dhey in-jee meh-tsahng, ngah-tso Phö-keh jahng thub-gi-ray

(here)(westerners)(not)(because),(we)(Tibetan)(practice)(can)

There are two useful structures introduced here. The first is the addition of *tsahng* to *meh* (or if it were a positive sentence, *yö*). This means "since" or "because" and refers to everything that precedes it—in this case: "Because there are no westerners...". If the phrase were *in-jee yö-tsahng* the meaning would have been "Because there are westerners...".

The second stucture, verb + *thub* + tense ending, means "to

be able". With a positive ending the meaning is that something
can be done, and with a negative that something cannot be done.

—For each night you must pay Y10.
   Tsen ray-ray la quai chu teh-goh-ray
   (night)(each)(each)(for)(coin)(10)(give)(need)

Outside Tibet, the word for money is *gor-mo*. We use the yuan
(pronounced *quai*) since these dialogues take place in Tibet. See
the introduction to SHOPPING for more information.

—But this Tibetan person only pays Y5.
   Yin-neh Phö-ba di quai ngah teh-gi-du
   (but) (Tibetan)(this)(coin)(5) (gives)

—Westerners must pay more.
   In-jee-tso mahng-wa teh-goh-ray
   (westerners) (more) (give)(need)

Mahng-wa is made from the adjective *mahng-bo* (much;many)
with the *bo* dropped and *wa* added.

—There is no difference between westerners and Tibetans.
   In-jee thang Phö-ba la kye-ba yo-mah-ray (*kye-ba*:difference)
   (westerners)(and)(Tibetans)(difference)(are not)

—Please take Y5.
   Quai ngah len-ro-nahng
   (coin) (5) (take)(please)

—I need a mattress.
   Ngah la bö-den goh
   (to me)(mattress)(need)

—Do you have hot water?
   Chu tsah-po yo-ray-peh
   (water)(hot) (have you)

—When can we get it?
   Kah-dü rah-gi-ray
   (when)(obtain)(will)

—In the afternoon between 4 and 6.
   Nying-ku chu-tsö shi-ba neh trook-ba phar-tu
   (afternoon)(hour) (4)   (from) (6)   (between)

Hours or locations + *phar-tu* mean between those times or locations.

—Do you have electricity and a shower?
  Keh-rahng la lohk thang sug-po tru-sah yö-peh
  (you) (electricity) (and) (body)(wash) (place) (have)

—We don't have a shower, but Kyiri Hotel does.
  Sug-po tru-sah meh. Yin-neh Kyi-ree dhön-khang la du
  (body)(wash)(place)(don't have)(but) '' (hotel) (at)(has)

—When are showers available there?
  Pha-ghey sug-po tru-sah kah-dü go che-gi-ray
  (there) (body) (wash) (when)(door)(open)(will)

—From 4 until 6 in the afternoon.
  Chu-tsö shi-ba neh trook-ba phar-tu
  (hour) (4) (from) (6) (between)

—Everyday?
  Nin-tahr?

—No, they are closed Sundays.
  Mah ray, sah nyi-ma la go gyahp-gi-ray
  (no), (Sunday) (at)(door)(closed)(on)

—How much does it cost?
  Kong kah-tsö ray
  (price)(how much)(is)

—Please show me where the bathroom is.
  Ngah la sahng-chö kah-bah yo-ray teh-ro-nahng
  (to me) (bathroom) (where) (is) (show)(please)

—Where are bicycles rented?
  Kahng-gah-ri kah-bah rah-gi-ray
  (bicycles) (where)(obtain)(will)

—We rent them here.
  Ngah-tsö dhey la-cha la teh-gi-yö
  (we) (here) (for rent) (give)

—Bicycles are rented at _____ (place).
Kahng-gah-ri _____ **la la-cha la rah-gi-ray**
(bicycles) _____ (at) (for rent) (obtain)(will)

—How much for an hour / the day / a week / one month?
Chu-tsö chik / nyi-ma chik / dün-tha chik / dah-wah chik
(hour) (one) / (day) (one) / (week) (one) / (month) (one)
la kha-tsö ray
(for)(how much)

10 Food

EATING AND DRINKING

If you visit a Tibetan family, there are a few customs you may want to be aware of. When a host offers food or drink to a guest, usually the guest will politely refuse a few times before indulging. The host might say: *shey shey* (please have some) and the guest would reply *la meh* (no thank-you) a few times. Don't say it in a harsh way or you may not be asked again!

You should consume much of what is offered but not all—if four pieces of bread are brought to be eaten, it's not uncommon to leave half a piece on the serving plate. You may be offered more food after the meal or snack, which you can politely refuse if nobody else is eating or your hosts appear poor. They may be offering you more food as a mere formality.

Tibetan tea (*Phö-cha*), a mixture of musky tea leaves, butter, and salt is a hot, broth-like beverage found in most Tibetan homes and restaurants. A host may pour you a cup, expect you to take a large drink, pour you a bit more, expect you to drink another sip, and top it off with another trickle. If you see people blowing on the tea, it's not to cool it off, rather to push away the butter that rises to the top.

Tibetan beer (*chahng*), made from fermented rice, barley, or other available grains, is found in abundance in Tibetan communities. You may be asked to join in some *chahng* drinking by the side of the road, in *chahng* houses, or with families. Though the taste might seem tame, it will catch up with you, so go easy at first if you indulge at all.

Roasted barley flour (*tsahm-pa*) is a staple food item for Tibetans. It is inexpensive, needs no cooking, and sits heavy in the belly to ward off the cold. Tibetans generally eat it two ways:

1) with just enough water and maybe some butter to mold it like clay (called *pahk*). It is squeezed in the hand with a closed fist so that the part between the forefinger and thumb is fat (the head), and the part coming out by the fifth finger is long and thin (the tail). This form of *tsahm-pa* is properly eaten from "head" to "tail".

2) mixed in a bowl with Tibetan tea, maybe some butter and sugar, and eaten like porridge (called *cham-du*).

Tibetans may feel that you, as a westerner, wouldn't like such food. In this case you should ask for some. They will enjoy sharing it with you, and eating *tsahm-pa* with Tibetans is a terrific way to break the ice.

RESTAURANT

Very few language skills are needed in a restaurant in Tibet. Restaurant proprietors know enough sign language and broken English to help you out. Many times you can just walk into the kitchen and point to what you want. Stir-fry meals are invented with the point of a finger, and all of the ingredients are immediately combined and cooked for you.

VOCABULARY

dairy foods: **kar-zeh**
  butter: **mahr**
  cheese: **chu-rah**
  curd: **sho**
  milk: **o-mah**

fruit: **shing-do**
  apple: **ku-shu**
  apricot: **nga-ri kham-bu**

grains: **tru-rik**
  barley/oats: **tru**
  corn: **ah-shom**
  rice: **dreh**
  wheat: **tro**

meat: **shah**
  yak meat: **yak shah**
  chicken: **cha shah**

grapes: **chu gun-drum**
orange: **tsha-lu-mah**
peach: **kham-bu**
pear: **li**

goat: **rah shah**
mutton: **luk shah**
pork: **pahk shah**
fish: **nyah shah**

drinks:
Tibetan tea: **Phö-cha**
sweet tea: **cha ngar-mo**
Tibetan beer: **chahng**
home-made alcohol: **ah-rah**
water: **chu**
hot boiled water:
        chu khö-mah
cold boiled water:
        chu khö-trahng

vegetables: **tshey**
bamboo shoot: **nyung-zah**
carrot: **kung la-bu**
lentil: **dah-li** (Hindi)
peas: **tre-ma**
potato: **sho-go**
radish: **la-bu**
spinach: **peh-tshey**
turnip: **nyung-ma**

Tibetan food:
steamed dumplings: **mo mo**
vegetarian dumplings: **mo mo shah meh-ba**
fried dumplings: **kah-tey**
fried meat patties: **sha pah-leh**
noodles in soup: **thook-pa**
egg noodles: **gyah-thook**
soybean noodles: **phing**
roasted barley flour: **tsahm-pa**
Tibetan cookies: **khap-say**
Tibetan bread: **pah-leh**

Tastes:

salt: **tsha**	—	salty: **tsha-gu**
sugar: **che-mah ka-ra**	—	sweet: **ngar-mo**
chili: **see-beh**	—	spicy: **kha tsah-po**

1) Where is there a ____?
  a) restaurant
  b) Tibetan restaurant
  c) western restaurant

_____ **kah-bah yo-ray**
  a) **sah-khang**
  b) **Phö-beh sah-khang**
  c) **in-jee sah-khang**

2) I have to eat ____.
   a) food
   b) breakfast
   c) lunch
   d) dinner

Ngah _____ sah-goh-yö
   a) kah-lah
   b) sho-gey kah-lah (or) sho-cha
   c) nying-ku kah-lah
   d) gong-tah kah-lah

3) I want ____.
   a) tea
   b) milk
   c) Tibetan tea
   d) an egg

Ngah la _____ goh
   a) cha
   b) o-mah
   c) Phö-cha
   d) go-ngah

4) This is _____ .
   a) hot
   b) cold
   c) fresh
   d) stale
   e) rotten
   f) sour

Di _____ du
   a) tsah-po
   b) trahng-mo
   c) sö-ba
   d) nying-ba
   e) roo-ba
   f) kyoor-mo

5) I am hungry.
   Ngah tro-go thö-gi-du
   (I) (hunger) (have)

6) I am thirsty.
   Ngah kha-kom-gi-du
   (I) (mouth)(dry)(have)

7) I like Tibetan food.
   Ngah Phö-beh kah-lah gah-bo yö
   (I) (Tibetan) (food) (like)(have)

8) Do you like Tibetan beer?
   Keh-rahng chahng la gah-bo yö-peh
   (you) (beer) (like) (have)

9) Let's go and drink some Tibetan beer.
   Ngah-tsö chahng thung-gah dro
   (we) (beer) (drink)(to)(go)

The suffix -*gah*, when attached to a verb means "in order to (verb)''. *Sah-gah dro* means ''Let's go (in order to) eat.''

10) Which restaurant has good food?
Sah-khang kah-gi la kah-lah yahk-po yo-ray
(restaurant)(which)(at)(food) (good) (has)

11) This food is too much for me.
Kah-lah di ngah la mahng-tahk du
(food) (this)(me)(for)(too much) (is)
The first syllable of some adjectives plus *tahk* means too much of that adjective. *Mahng-tahk*, above,is the word *mahng-bo* (many) less the *bo* suffix, plus *tahk*.

12) Enough / I'm full.   (This can be used for food
Dik song   or drink, or to mean ''I'm
    satisfied''. If you are not full or
    satisfied you would say *dik mah-song*)

13) I don't eat meat.
Ngah shah sah-gi-meh
(I)   (meat) (eat)(will not)

By saying that you want a vegetable meal (*tshey gi* + whatever dish), there is no guarantee that meat will not be included with the vegetables. However, by saying that you want a particular dish without meat (whatever dish + *shah meh-ba*) you have a better chance of receiving a purely vegetarian meal.

RESTAURANT DIALOGUE

—Do you have dumplings / vegetarian dumplings?
Mo mo / mo mo shah meh-ba yö-peh
(dumplings)/(dumplings)(meat)(without)(have you)
The noun + *meh-ba* means ''without the (noun)''. So *shah meh-ba* means ''without meat''.

—Do you have meat or fish today?
Thi-ring shah yö, nyah yö
(today) (meat), (fish)(have you)
There is no word for ''or'' in common spoken Tibetan. It is im-

plied by the use of pauses and tones. Listen closely to the tape at sentences where "or" is used. The sentence above and the one below are good examples.

—No, we are all out/Yes, one plate or two?
Meh, tsahng-ma zoh song / Yó, tha-ba chik goh, nyi goh
(no) (all) (finished) / (yes) (plate) (one)(need)(two)(need)

—What kind of meat do you have today?
Thi-ring kah-rey gi shah yö
(today) (what) (of)(meat)(have)

—Today we have chicken, it's (very) fresh.
Thi-ring cha-shah yö, sö-ba ray
(today)(chicken)(meat)(have),(fresh)(is)

—Bring me noodles in soup / soup without meat.
Ngah la thook-ba / thook-ba shah meh-ba teh-ro-nahng
(to me) (soup) / (soup) (meat) (without) (give)(please)

—Do you have meat patties?
Shah pah-leh yö-peh
(meat)(bread)(have you)

—I didn't order this.
Ngey di ngah meh
(I) (this)(order)(not)

—Bring another one/ More of the same.
Shen-da chik kye-sho / Tah-gah-nahng-shin kye-sho
(another)(one)(bring)(come) / (just like) (bring)(come)

Both the command endings *ro-nahng* and *sho* have been used in this dialogue. The former is more polite and formal while the latter, though it could be considered a strong command in some situations, is merely informal and casual.

The phrase *tah-gah-nahng-shin* is very useful and means "just like that."

—Another Tibetan tea, please.
Phö-cha than-do chik teh-ro-nahng
(Tibetan tea)(more)(one)(give)(please)

—How much is the bill?
Ngü kah-tsö ray
(money)(how much)(is)

—This restaurant is inexpensive/ expensive.
Sah-khang di kong choong choong / kong chen-po du
(restaurant)(this)(price) (small) / (price) (large) (is)

11 Shopping

At the time of publication there are rumors that the Foreign Exchange Certificates (FEC), the tourist money in Tibet, will be discontinued. Even if it is not, it's best to exchange your FEC's for the "People's Money," Renminbi, especially if you plan to buy things in the bazaar. This way you will not only be speaking their language but trading with their money, too.

The yuan is called "quai" or *gormo chik*. (In Nepal, *gormo chik* refers to one Nepali rupee.) In Tibet the quai is divided into ten mao (called *mo-tse*), so that fifty mao equal *gormo che-kah* (half a quai). See NUMBERS in the back of the book for a complete number list.

You may wish to purchase many things at bazaars in Tibet, but remember that if what you buy looks too old or valuable, the items may be confiscated as you leave the country. In some instances "old" means pre-1959.

Don't be shy to bargain on the price of an item or trade it for something you have. Do some shopping around to find out the going price, and remember that almost anything from the West is considered valuable. A good way to practice and learn vocabulary is to ask a salesperson the name of an item and its price. This way the names of things will become engrained in your memory as will the sounds of numbers and prices.

Sometimes salespeople will bite stones to show you they are real. To test for true amber they will rub it on the back of their hand or arm—real amber lets off a musky, resin-like smell when rubbed in this way. And it is said that if you wrap a single human hair around a piece of real ivory, it will not burn if touched by a lit match.

VOCABULARY

Merchandise at the Bazaar

altar bowl: **teeng**
amber: **po-shi**
apron: **pahng-den**
belt: **keh-ra**
bell: **tril-bu**
blanket: **nye-jeh**
butter lamp: **chö-may**
carpet: **den**
conch shell: **dhoong**
coral: **che-roo**
drum: **dah-ma-ru**
hat: **shah-mo**
knife: **thi** / religious
   dagger: **phur-ba**
ladies dress/man's coat:
   chu-ba
mask: **bahk**
pants: **khu-doong**
prayer flag: **thar-cho**
religious book: **peh-cha**
religious painting: **thang-ka**
religious scarf: **kah-tah**
rosary: **treng-ah**
scarf: **kah-ti**
shirt: **tu-toong/wahn-joo**

Materials

bone: **roo-ko**
brass: **sahng**
bronze: **lee**
copper: **rah**
cotton: **reh**
crystal: **shel**
diamond: **pha-lahm**
gold: **ser**
ivory: **phe-so**
metal: **chah**
mother of pearl: **mo-tee**
porcelain: **kah-yul**
silk: **thu-chi**
silver: **ngü**
skin: **pahk-pa**
wool: **phel**

———

shoes: **hahng-go**
statue: **ku**
turquoise: **yoo**
vajra: **dor-jeh**
(blessed) water vessel:
   poom-ba
zee stone: **zee**

The last item, the zee stone—a brown agate—is extremely valuable to Tibetans. Circles on the stone are called "eyes" and help determine its value. The smaller the odd-number of eyes found on a stone, the more valuable it is. A three-eyed zee is more valuable than a four-eyed zee. However, a real stone is difficult to discern from a fake.

USEFUL PHRASES

1) What's the meaning of this _____?
   _____ **Di gi tön-tah kah-rey ray**
   a) mask
   a) **bahk**
   b) religious painting
   b) **thang-ka**
   c) *mandala*
   c) **kyil-khor**

2) How much is it?
   Kong kah-tsö ray

3) Make it less please.
   Kong chahk-ro-nahng

4) These together are how much?
   Di tsahng-ma kah-tsö ray

5) I'll trade you this __.
   __ **jeh-bu gyahp gi-yin**

6) That _____doesn't look real.
   Di ___ ngu-ney gi nahng-shin min-du
   a) turquoise
   a) **yoo**
   b) amber
   b) **po-shi**
   c) coral
   c) **che-roo**

7) Do you have a____ one?
   Keh-rahng la___ yö-peh
   a) better
   a) **yah-gan**
   b) cheaper
   b) **kong chu-ngah**
   c) newer
   c) **sah-rah**
   d) older
   d) **nying-ngah**
   e) thicker
   e) **thoo-pa**
   f) thinner
   f) **tha-wa**

8) This is too _____.
   Di ___ du
   a) big
   a) **che-tahk**
   b) small
   b) **choong-tahk**
   c) expensive
   c) **kong che-tahk**
   d) old
   d) **nying-tahk**

9) Is this ____?   **Di** ____ **ray-peh**
   a) gold   a) **ser**
   b) silver   b) **ngü**
   c) old   c) **nying-ba**
   d) new   d) **sar-pa**

MARKET DIALOGUE

—What would you like to buy?
  Keh-rahng kah-rey nyo-geh
  (you)   (what) (buy)(will)

—What is this?
  Di kah-rey ray
  (this)(what)(is)

—This is a dagger/Tibetan knife/butter lamp.
  Di phur-ba / thi / chö-may / ray
  (this)(dagger)/(knife)/(butter lamp)/ (is)

—Is it old or new?
  Sar-pa ray, nying-pa ray   (Again, listen for the tone of
  (new) (is)   (old) (is)   voice in the tape that
                                  signifies ''or'')

—Of what is it made? (or) What material is it?
  Di kah-rey gi sö-pah-ray (or) **Di gi gyup-cha kah-rey ray**
  (it)(what)(of) (was made) / (this)(material) (what) (is)

—How much is it?
  Kong kah-tsö ray
  (price)(how much)(is it)

—It is 50 rupees.
  Di gor-mo ngah-chu ray
  (this)(coins) (50)   (is)

—That's too expensive/That's cheap.
  Kong chen-po ray/kong choong choong ray
  (price)(much)(is) / (price) (little)   (is)

—Do you have cheaper/better ones?
Kong chu-ngah / yah-gah yö-peh
(price) (less) / (better)(do you have)

—Show me those rosaries/necklaces over there.
Ngah-la treng-ah / kye-gen phan-tso teh-ro-nahng
(to me) (rosary) / (necklace) (those) (show please)

—What stone are they?
Tha   kah-rey   ray
(precious stone)(what) (is)

—They are turquoise/coral/amber/ivory.
Phan-tso yoo / che-roo / po-shi / phe-so ray
(those)(turquoise)/   (coral) / (amber) / (ivory)(are)

—Are the stones real?
Tha ngu-ney gi ray-peh   (or)   **Tha din-tso tha rahng ray-peh**
(stone)(real)(of)(are they)   (stone)(these)(stone)(real)(are they)

—Yes, they are authentic.   (*ngoh-ma*: authentic)
La ray, ngoh-ma ray
(yes) (authentic)(are)

—Is the ivory real too?
Phe-so di yeh ngu-ney gi ray-peh
(ivory)(this)(also)(real) (of) (is it)

—Yes, it is Chinese ivory.
La ray, Gyah-mi gi phe-so ray
(yes) (Chinese) (of) (ivory) (is)

—How much is it?
Kah-tsö ray
(how much)(is)

—I don't have that much money. Please make it cheaper.
Ngah la ngü mahng-bo meh.   Kong chahk-ro-nang
(to me) (money)(much)(don't have).(price)(less)(please)

—Who is that a statue of?
Ku pha-ghey su ray
(statue)(there) (who) (is)

—That is Chenrezi / the goddess Tara(green or white) / Guru Rinpoche.

Pha-ghey Chen-reh-zi / Dro-ma (jang-gu;kahr-po) /
(that)(the deity Chenrezi)/(the goddess Tara (white;green)/
Guru Rin-po-chay gi ray
(Guru Rinpoche) (of) (is)

These deities are explained in the MONASTERY DIALOGUE.

—Do you have robes?   (The word *chuba* is used for Tibetan
Chu-ba yö-peh   gowns, robes worn by both men
(chuba)(have you)   and women)

—Like this?
Di nahng-shin
(this)(just like)

—No, not that kind. A thinner / thicker one.
Di nahng-shin mah-ray. Thoo-pa / tha-wa chik
(this)(just like) (not)   (thicker) / (thinner)(one)

—Is this religious painting real or fake?/It looks fake.
Thang-ka di ngoh-ma ray, zoo-ma ray /Zoo-ma nahng-shin du
(painting)(this)(real) (is), (fake) (is) / (fake) (just like) (is)

—How much is this all together?
Di tsahng-ma kah-tsö ray
(this) (all) (how much) (is)

—I'll give you _____ amount for everything.
Ngah cha-la tsahng-ma la gor-mo _____ teh-gi-yin
(I) (things) (all)   (for)(coins) _____ (give)(will)

—I'll trade you this watch for everything.
Ngah chu-tsö di cha-la tsahng-ma nyem-do jeh-bu gyahp-gi-yin
(I) (watch)(this)(things) (all)   (for)   (trade) (will)

—Your watch and 100 rupees and it's okay with me.
Chu-tsö thang gor-mo gyah teh-nah di-gi-ray
(watch) (and) (coins)(100) (give)(if)(okay)(is)

12 Monastic Dialogues

Don't be afraid to visit monasteries. They are the hub of religious and secular life for Tibetans—housing fantastic and artistic items, as well as a living religious tradition. Always walk around shrines or altars in a clockwise manner, passing anything sacred on your right. If in doubt, follow the examples of others.

It is best to dress with some respect when visiting a monastery. Short pants are not recommended to be worn by either men or women. If there happens to be a ceremony in progress, don't hesitate to enter unless told otherwise. Also, don't be surprised if your few words of Tibetan get you spontaneous invitations to drink tea, share a meal, or enter rooms usually off-limits to tourists.

For detailed information on what you may see and hear in a monastery, consult the RELIGIOUS AND MONASTIC VOCABULARY in the appendix.

Dalai Lama Pictures

Many people visiting Tibet stock up on pictures of the Dalai Lama, Tibet's temporal and spiritual leader in exile. They are being used to barter for goods, get access to difficult to enter areas, in exchange for the right to photograph within monasteries, and just to give away at random.

With Dalai Lama pictures being given out so freely, a business of sorts has begun where pictures are being sold to vendors, who sell them to tourists, who give them to whomever asks, who sell them back to the vendors. However, there are those who value a Dalai Lama picture beyond its monetary worth. Not only for this reason is it advisable to be discreet when handing out such photos, but for personal safety as well. You are likely to be physically mobbed if you start handing out such photos at random.

USEFUL PHRASES

1) May I _____ ?
   a) come inside
   b) take a picture
   c) wear my shoes

_____ **cho-gi-ray-peh**
   a) **bu la yong**
   b) **pahr gyahp**
   c) **hahng-go khön**

2) These people are ____ .
   a) praying
   b) prostrating
   c) circumambulating
   d) offering butter lamps

Mi din-tso _____ **gi-du**
   a) **mu-lahm gyahp**
   b) **cha-tsel**
   c) **ko-rah gyahp**
   d) **chö-may phul**

3) May I offer ____ ?
   a) incense
   b) money
   c) butter lamps
   d) (a) white scarf

____ **phul-nah di-gi-ray-peh**
   a) **pö**
   b) **ngü**
   c) **chö-may**
   d) **kah-tah**

4) Where is (are) the ____ ?
   a) altar
   b) lama's throne
   c) statues
   d) religious painting

____ **kah-bah yo-ray**
   a) **chö-shum**
   b) **la-ma gi shug-ti**
   c) **ku**
   d) **thang-ka**

5)   Of whom is this statue?
   Di su ku ray   (or)   **Ku di su ray**
   (this)(who)(statue)(is)   (statue)(this)(who)(is)

6)   What is the meaning of this _____ ?
   _____ **di gi tön-tah kah-rey ray**
   _____(this)(of)(meaning)(what)(is)

GENERAL MONASTIC DIALOGUE

—Don't enter with your shoes on.
Hahng-go khön-neh dro cho-gi-mah-ray
(shoes)   (wear)(since)(go)(not allowed)
In Tibet, shoes are worn in the monasteries. In Nepal and India
they are usually not.

—Put them outside.
Hahng-go chi-la shah
(shoes) (outside) (put)

—May I come in now?
Than-dah bu la yong-nah di-gi-ray-peh
(now)   (inside) (come)(if) (is it alright)
You can also say *nahng la* to mean "inside".

—Yes, please come in.
La ray, yah phe
(yes)   (come)(please)
Yah phe is often heard and means "Please come here", or "Please
come in".

—What are those people doing?
Mi din-tso kah-rey che-gi-yo-ray
(people)(those)(what)(doing)(are)

—They are prostrating.   (see explanation in the
Khong-tso cha-tsel gi-yo-ray   RELIGIOUS AND MON-
(they)(prostrating)(are)   ASTIC VOCABULARY
                                                                appendix)

—It is a Tibetan Buddhist custom.
Nahng-peh luk-sül ray
(Tibetan Buddhist)(custom)(is)

—What are those scarves?
Kha-ti phan-tso kah-rey ray
(scarves) (those) (what) (are)

—They are called *kata*. They are offered to the deities.
Phan-tso kah-tah ray. Lha thang lha-mo la phul-gi-ray
(they)   "   (are).(god)(and)(goddess)(to)(give)(are)

Phul is the honorific form of the verb "give"(*teh*). Using it shows respect to whom something is offered.

—Where do you get *katas*?
Kah-tah kah-bah rah-gi-ray
    "   (where) (obtain)(are)

—At the market, or sometimes we sell them here.
Trom la, yin-neh kahp kahp-la ngah-tsö dhey tsong-gi-yö
(market)(at)(but) (sometimes)   (we)   (here)(selling)(are)

—I don't have a *kata* to offer.
Ngah la kah-tah phul-yah meh
(to me)   "   (to give)(don't have)
The use of *-yah* here is a gerund form, as explained earlier.

—It doesn't matter, you can offer a few coins if you want.
Keh che-gi-mah-ray, ngü phul-nah di-gi-ray
(important) (not), (coin) (give)(if) (okay)
    (*keh che-gi-mah-ray*: it doesn't matter)

—What's that sound?
Keh di kah-rey ray
(voice)(that)(what)(is)

—People are saying *mantras*. (see explanation in back of the book)
Mi-tsö mah-ni dahng-gi-yo-ray
(people)(*mantra*)(saying)(are)

—I can't see those wall paintings.
Thang-ka phan-tso thong-gi-min-du
(painting) (those)   (see)   (not)

—Did you bring your flashlight?
Keh-rahng lohk-shu kye-yö-peh
(you)   (lamp) (bring)(have)

—Yes / No, I forgot it.
Yö / Meh, ngey jeh-song
(yes)/(no) (I)   (forgot)

—Shine it on the wall and you will see clearly.
Tsik-pa la shu-ma teh-nah a-ni sel-po thong-gi-ray
(wall) (on) (lamp) (show)(if)(and)(clearly)(see)(will)

—There are many people here.
Dhey mi mahng-bo du
(here)(people)(many)(are)

—In the morning many people come.
Ngah-toh mi mahng-bo yong-gi-ray
(morning)(people)(many) (come)

—I'm thirsty.
Ngah kha-kohm-gi-du
(I)   (thirsty) (am)

—Do you have water?
Chu yö-peh
(water)(have)

—Yes, in my waterbottle.
La yö, chu gi she-tham la
(yes) (water)(of)(flask)(in)

—Please come over here, sit down, and have some tea.
Dhey phe-ro-nahng,   shoo,   cha shey.
(here)(come)(please),(please sit),(tea)(please have)
Note the honorific uses of "come" (*phe*), "sit" (*shoo*), and "consume" (*shey*).

—I have no cup.
Ngah la kah-yul meh
(to me) (cup) (have not)

—We have many here.
Dhey mahng-bo yö
(here)(many)(have)

—Do you like Tibetan tea?
Keh-rahng Phö-cha la gah-bo yö-peh
(you) (Tibetan tea)(to)(like)(have)

—I've never tried it.

Ngey kah-dü-yeh (accent middle syllable) **thung-meh**

  (I)   (never)   (drink)(have not)

Again, "never" is constructed by using *kah-dü-yeh* plus a negative verb.

—Have some it's good.

De-tsi shey, shim-bu yo-ray

(a little)(have)(delicious)(is)

—Do you live here?

Keh-rahng dhey shoo-gi-yö-peh

(you)   (here) (stay) (are)

—Yes, I'm one of a few monks who live here.

La yö, ngah thang ku-sho kah-shey nyem-do deh-gi-yö

(yes), (I) (and) (monks) (several) (with)   (stay)(am)

Note how the honorific *shoo* changed to *deh* when the monk spoke about himself.

—Do you have ceremonies here?

Dhey shap-den che-gi-yo-ray-peh

(here)(ceremony)(doing) (are you)

—Yes, on the full moon.

La yo-ray, tse-ba chu-ngah la

(yes)(have),(date) (fifteen) (on)

The fifteenth day of the lunar calendar is the full moon. See DATES AND DAYS.

—May I come at that time?

De-thu yong-nah di-gi-ray-peh

(that time)(come)(if)(is it okay)

—Yes. You cannot take pictures but you will receive special food.

Di-gi-ray. Keh-rahng pahr gyahp cho-gi-mah-ray, yin-neh tsok

(it's okay).(you)   (photograph) (can't), (but)(special food)

rah-gi-ray

(obtain)(will)

—What is *tsok*?

Tsok kah-rey ray

   "   (what) (is)

—It is blessed food. (blessed by a deity or lama)
Tsok chin-lahp ray
  '' (blessed food)(is)

—What sect is this monastery?
Gom-pa di gi chö-luk kah-gi ray
(monastery)(this)(sect) (which)(is)

—We are Kagyu / Nyingma / Gelug / Sakya.
Ngah-tsö Kah-gyu / Nying-ma / Geh-lug / Sah-kya yin
(we)   ''   ''   ''   '' (are)
These are the four major sects of Tibetan Buddhism.

—Do many westerners come here?
Dhey in-jee mahng-bo yong-gi-ray-peh
(here)(westerner)(many)(come)(are)

—Yes. They all take a lot of pictures.
La ray. Khon-tso pahr mahng-bo gyahp-gi-ray
(yes). (they)   (pictures)(many) (take) (are)
The verb "photograph" is the type of verb talked about in the
SYLLABLE COMBINING section. Any modifier of the verb
is placed between the noun and actual verb particle:
pahr gyahp: photograph   *pahr mahng-bo gyahp*: many photographs

—You must give money for photographs taken.
Pahr-gyahp yah-la ngü teh-goh-ray
(photograph) (for) (money)(give)(need)

—Can people photograph from outside for free?
Chi-neh,   ngü mah-teh-pa pahr gyahp cho-gi-ray-peh
(outside)(from)(money)(not give)(photograph)(is it allowed)

—Yes, they can.
Cho-gi-ray
(it is allowed)

—I have a camera. May I take a picture?
Ngah la pahr-che yö. Pahr gyahp-nah di-gi-ray-peh
(I)   (camera)(have). (photograph) (if)(is it alright)

—Yes. You don't need to pay.
Di-gi-ray.   Ngü teh-goh-mah-ray
(it's alright)(money)(give)(not need)

—You are just like a Tibetan; you speak so well.
**Keh-rahng Phö-ba nahng-shin du; Phö-keh yahk-po
gyahp-gi-du**
(you)   (Tibetan) (just like)(are); (Tibetan)(well)
(speak)
Here is another case of a two-part verb. The modifier *yahk-po*
falls between *Phö-keh* (Tibetan language) and *gyahp* ("do"—or,
in this case, "speak").

—No, I don't know Tibetan well at all.
La meh, ngah Phö-keh yahk-po shing-gi-meh
(No),   (I)   (Tibetan)   (well)   (know) (not)

—Don't say that. Slowly, slowly you will learn.
Mah-soong. Kah-leh, kah-leh la jahng-gi-ray
(don't)(say). (slowly) (slowly)   (learn) (will)
Soong is the honorific form of *lahp* ("talk").

—Please take a picture of us
Ngah-tsö pahr gyahp-ro-nahng
(us)   (photograph) (please)

—Okay. Don't move.
Lah-so.   Khoo-kyok   mah-tahng
(okay). (here and there)(don't move)

—Send it to us (when it is developed).
Ngah-tso la pahr tahng-ro-nahng
(us)   (to) (picture) (send)(please)

—Write your name and address on this paper.
Keh-rahng gi ming thang kha-jahng shu-gu di la thi-ro-nahng
(you)   (of)(name)(and)(address)(paper)(this)(on)(write)(please)

—When will you send it?
Kah-dü tahng-gi-yin-peh
(when) (send)(will)(you)

—Not immediately. Two or three months.
Lahm-sahng tahng-gi-meh. Dah-wah chik, nyi, gi shoog-la
(immediately)(send)(will not). (month) (one),(two),(after)

—Is there a lama here now?
La-ma shoo-du-geh
    "   (stay) (is)

—Not now, he just left.
Than-dah shoo-min-du, phe-song
(now)   (stay)(not),   (went:honorific)

—I want to visit some holy places.
Ngah sah-cha tsa-chen-po la dron-dö-yö
(I)   (place)   (powerful) (to) (go) (want)
Again, note the use of *dö*. The verb (*dro*) takes on the ''n'' suffix
(*dro + n*) when this form is used.

—Do you know of some?
Keh-rahng sah-cha tsa-chen-po shing-gi-yö-peh
(you)   (places)   (powerful)   (know)(have)

—There are several caves around here.
Di-bah la (accent middle syllable) **trah-pu kah-shey yo-ray**
(around here)   (cave) (several) (are)

—One is west of Nedong. It takes about 4 or 5 hours to walk.
Chik Neh-dong neh noop chok la yo-ray. Khom-ba gyahp-nah
(one)   "   (from)(west)   (is).   (walk) (if)
chu-tsö shi, ngah goh-gi-ray
(hour) (4), (5)   (need)
Again, listen for the pauses that signify the ''or'' in the sentence.

—It's called Sheta Monastery.
Sah-cha gi ming la She-tah Gom-pa ray
(place)(of)(name)   "   (monastery)(is)
This is located on top of Sheta Mountain, across the valley from
Nedong.

—May I look at the altar / those statues?
Ngah chö-sahm / ku phan-tso la tah-nah di-gi-ray-peh
(I)   (altar) / (statues)(those) (at) (look)(if) (is it alright)

—What statue is that?
Ku pha-ghey su ray
(statue)(that)(who)(is)

—That is Green Tara.
Pha-ghey Dro-ma ray
(that)　(Tara)　(is)

Tara is a popular goddess/deity in Tibet, found both in white and green manifestations.

—Is this trumpet made from a ram's bone?
Thung-chen di luk gi roo-ko gi sö-pah-ray-peh
(horn)　　(this)(ram)(of)(bone)(of)(made)(is it)

—No, it is human.
Mah-ray, mi gi roo-ko ray
(no) ,　(human)(of)(bone)(is)

—No kidding?
Ngu-ney

—I must go now.
Tha, ngah dro-goh-yö
(now),　(I)　(go)(need)

—Okay, see you soon.
Lah-so, gyok-po jeh-yong
(okay)　(soon)　(meet)(come)

JOKHANG

The Jokhang is the spiritual hub of Lhasa. Built in the 7th century by the king who helped bring Buddhism to Tibet, the Jokhang is constantly surrounded by devout worshippers and prostrating pilgrims. This is a wonderful place to get a true and immediate sense of what Tibetans and their religion are all about.

JOKHANG DIALOGUE

—What time does the Jokhang open?
Jo-khang chu-tsö kah-tsö la che-gi-ray
　　"　　(time)　(what)　(at) (will open)

—About nine in the morning.
Chu-tsö gu-ba tsah la   (*tsah* is the shortened version
(o'clock)(nine)(about)(at)   of *tsahm la* meaning "about")

—Go early before the pilgrims rush in.
Ngah-bo gyu, neh-kor-ken mah-yong kong-la
(early) (go) (pilgrims)   (not)(come)(before)
"Before" is designated by a negative particle + verb root +
kong-la.
a) Before she arrived... = **Khong mah-lep kong-la...**
b) Before we drank tea... = **Ngah-tso cha mah-thung kong-la...**

—Look at all the people!
Mi tsahng-ma la tah-nahng!
(people)(all)   (at)   (look)

—They are circumambulating the temple.
Khong-tso lha-khang la ko-rah gyahp-gi-du
(they)   (temple)   (at) (circumambulating)

—Over here people are selling goods.
Dhey mi-tso cha-la tsong-gi-du
(here)(people)(things)(selling)

—The doors are opening now.
Than-dah go che-gi-du
(now)   (doors)(opening)

—Watch out!
Cha-gah chi!

—Everyone is pushing.
Mi tsahng-ma bi-gyah gyahp-gi-du
(people)(all)   (pushing)   (are)

—Where is Jowo Rinpoche?
Jo-woh Rin-po-chay kah-bah yo-ray
   "   "   (where) (is)

—Directly in the back.
Kha-too, gyahp-lo la
(straight) (in the back)

—May I go upstairs?
Ngah tho-gah la dro cho-gi-ray-peh
(I) (upstairs)(to)(go)(is it allowed)

—Yes, you may / No, you may not.
Cho-gi-ray / Cho-gi-mah-ray
(you are allowed)/(you are not allowed)

—Where is the Palden Lhamo?
Pal-den Lha-mo kah-bah yo-ray
"   "   (where) (is)

—When do you close?
Kah-dü go gyahp-gi-ray
(when)(door)(close)(will)

—At one o'clock.
Chu-tsö chik la
(o'clock)(one)(at)

—Can I come back after one o'clock?
Chu-tsö chik gi jeh-la yong-nah di-gi-ray-peh
(o'clock)(one) (after) (come)(if) (is it okay)

—It's alright.
Di-gi-ray

Since less people visit the Jokhang in the afternoon, this is a good
time to speak with the monks and receive an informal tour of
the temple. Also, every evening religious ceremonies are performed there.

—What is that man doing?
Mi pha-ghey kah-rey che-gi-yo-ray
(man) (that) (what) (doing)

—He's writing prayers for people.
Khong mi-tso la mu-lahm thi-gi-du
(he) (people)(for)(prayers) (writes)

—How (in what manner)?
Kahn-dre-si

—He writes people's names into the prayer.
Mu-lahm la mi-gi-ming thi-gi-yo-ray
(prayers)(in)(people's names)(writes)

—Can I give him a western name?
In-jee ming teh-nah di-gi-ray-peh
(western)(name)(give)(if)(is it okay)

—It's okay.
Di-gi-ray

For a small fee this fellow will write names of either living or dead persons into prayers. According to Tibetan Buddhist belief, this produces merit for them even if they are dead.

DREPUNG

Literally "rice heap," and once the largest monastery in Tibet, Drepung is slowly rebuilding after suffering great destruction in 1959. It lies slightly north and about five miles west of Lhasa. You will pass what was once the State Oracle's home, Nechung Monastery, on the way to Drepung.

DREPUNG DIALOGUE

—Where is Drepung from here?
Di neh Dreh-pung kah-bah yo-ray
(from here) " (where) (is)

—Over there a short distance.
Yah-ghey, tha ring-bo shi-tah yo-mah-ray
(up over there),(distance)(long)(much)(is not)

—Can I walk there?
Khom-ba gyahp-nah lep-gi-ray-peh
(walk) (if)(arrive)(will)

—If you walk, it will take (about) two hours.
Khom-ba gyahp-nah chu-tsö nyi goh-gi-ray
(walk) (if) (hour) (two)(need)(will)

—It's better if you ride a bicycle.
Kahng-gah-ri la chin-nah yahg-gi-ray
(bicycle)   (to) (went)(if)(better)(will be)

—Do busses go there?
Pha-ghey lahm-khor dro-gi-ray-peh
(there)   (busses) (going) (are)

—Yes, twice daily.
Dro-gi-ray, nyi-ma chik la theng nyi   (*theng*: times)
(will go) (day) (one)(in)(times)(two)

—What temple is that?
Pha-ghey lha-khang kah-gi ray
(that)   (temple) (which) (is)

—That's Nechung temple.   (This was once home of the
Pha-ghey Neh-chung lha-khang ray   famous oracle whose
(that)   "   (temple) (is)   prophecies were held
in high regard by the
ruling administrators)

—Where does this path lead?
Lahm-kah di kah-bah dro-gi-ray
(road)   (this)(where)(goes)

—To the main chanting hall of Loseling.
Lo-seh-ling gi thön-khang la
"   (of)(chanting hall) (to)

—Many buildings have been destroyed.
Khang-pa mahng-bo meh-ba sö yo-ray
(buildings)(many)   (without) (made)(are)

—Yes, but they are slowly rebuilding.
Ray, yin-neh kah-leh la sö-kyor gyahp-gi-yo-ray
(yes)(but)   (slowly) (rebuilding) (are)

—If you climb these stairs, you'll go up to the roof.
Ken-zah din-tso zah-nah, tho-gah la lep-gi-ray
(stairs) (these) (climb)(if) (roof)   (arrive)(will)

—Is this the kitchen?
Di thap-tsahng ray-peh
(this)(kitchen)(is it)

—How many monks used to live here?
Ngeh-ma dhey tra-pa kah-tsö deh-pah-ray
(before) (here)(monks)(how many)(stayed)

—About 6000.
Trook-tong tsah
(six)(thousand)(about)

—How many are here these days?
Thi-ring-sahng kah-tsö yo-ray   (*thi-ring-sahng*:
(these days) (how many)(are)   "these days")

—I'm not sure, but not many.
Ngah ten-den meh, yin-neh mahng-bo yo-mah-ray
(I) (sure) (not) (but) (many) (are not)

—Those monks are performing a ceremony.
Ku-sho phan-tso shap-den che-gi-du
(monks)(those) (ceremony) (doing)

—Where is the Tsug-gyen College?
Tsug-gyen thu-rim lahp-tha kah-bah yo-ray
    "   (college)   (where) (is)

—I heard there is a huge religious painting there.
Pha-ghey thang-ka chen-po chik yo-ray, koh-chung
(there)(religious painting)(big)(one)(is) , (I heard)
Note the use of "hear". You say the item that you heard, and
add *koh-chung* or *koh-song*. This means that you heard everything
preceding *koh-chung* or *koh-song*.

—Yes, there is. It is located just behind the Loseling.
La, yo-ray. Lo-seh-ling gi gyahp-lo-la yo-ray
(yes) (is).   "   (behind)   (is)

SERA

The name Sera ("hail") is significant in understanding its com-
petitive reputation with Drepung Monastery ("rice heap"), since

hail destroys rice. Smaller than Drepung, Sera is located about three miles north of Lhasa. In the vicinity of the monastery are deities and historical figures painted on rock faces, as well as a location for sky burial.

Sky Burials

These sites are located at places away from congested areas. Bodies are cut into pieces there, and left for vultures to consume. In the past, westerners found these spots particularly interesting but their photographic efforts caused tension among family members of the deceased. Not only did death become sensationalized, but photography was said to interfere with the soul's release from the body.

Sky burial locations were then made off-limits to westerners. However, many continue to sneak around and watch or photograph, causing still greater tension. We highly recommend that you stay clear of these areas.

SERA DIALOGUE

—Where is Sera from here (Lhasa)?
Sera, (Lhasa) neh kah-bah yo-ray
    ”   ”   (from)(where)(is)

—Go directly north.
Chang-chok la kha-too gyu
(north)   (to)(directly)(go)

—Do busses go there?
Pha-ghey lahm-khor dro-gi-ray-peh
(there)   (busses)   (going)

—Yes, or hitch a ride on any vehicle going that way.
Dro-gi-ray, yah-meh-nah mo-tah gi kye rog-che-gi-ray
(they go), (otherwise) (auto) (bring) (help) (will)

—Is this where they have debates?
Di tsö-ba gyahp-sah ray-peh
(this)(debate)(place)(is it)

—Where are the rock paintings?

Doh la ti-beh ri-mo kah-bah yo-ray

(rock) (painted) (where) (are)

—They are just east of here, against the mountain.

Di neh noop-chok la, kahng-ree la

(from here)(east) (is), (mountain)(at)

—What deities are depicted there?

Pha-ghey lha thang lha-mo su su yo-ray

(there) (gods)(and)(goddesses)(who all)(are)

Su repeated twice here means: specifically which deities are depicted. You can double other words for the same effect: *kah-bah kah-bah* means "where exactly".

—Among the statues there are a large Yamantaka and a Tsong Khapa.

Ku nahng la Dor-jeh Jig-jeh chik thang Tsong Kha-pa chik

(statues)(among) (Yamantaka)(one)(and) '' '' (one)

yo-ray

(are)

Yamantaka, Slayer of Death, is a wrathful deity in the Tibetan Buddhist pantheon, and Tsong Khapa was a fourteenth-century reformer who founded the Gelugpa sect of Tibetan Buddhism.

—What else should I see at Sera?

Sera la shen-da kah-rey tah-ya yo-ray

'' (at)(other) (what) (to see) (is)

—From the area of the rock paintings, you can enter the chanting hall from the roof.

Doh-la ri-mo yö-sah neh,   thon-khang la zoo-gi-ray

(rock of)(painting)(place)(from)(chanting hall)(to)(enter)(will)

—Inside there are two statues, one Avalokiteshwara and one Maitreya.

Nahng la ku nyi yo-ray,   chik Chen-reh-zi thang chik

(inside)(statues)(two)(are), (one) '' (and) (one)

Cham-pa gi ray

'' (are)

Avalokiteshwara is the Deity of Compassion and Maitreya is the Buddha to Come. Both names are in Sanskrit.

—I heard there are a nunnery and hermits' caves near Sera.
Ngey Sera gi thi-la ah-ni gom-pa thang gom-chen gi trah-pu
(I) '' (near) (nunnery) (and) (hermit) (of) (cave)
yo-ray, koh-song
(are) , (heard)
Again, the use of "I" + information + *koh-song* means that you heard the information. Sometimes instead of *koh-song* you will hear *koh-chung*.

—Yes, I have heard that too.
La ray, ngey yeh koh-chung
(yes) (I) (also)(heard)

—Have you been there before?
Keh-rahng pha-ghey dro nyung-ngey
(you) (there) (go) (have experienced)

Nyung-ngey is slightly difficult to pronounce. The *ny* is pronounced like the Russian *nyet*, and the *ng* is pronounced as described in the phonetic system. This form can be used in a variety of situations: "have you eaten this before?" (*di sah nyung-ngey*), "have you seen this before?" (*di thong nyung-ngey*) and so on. The *ngey* suffix is the question particle. Just drop that to form an affirmative response, and add *mah* to *nyung* in the negative.

—No, not yet.
La meh, than-dah dro-mah-nyung
(no) (now) (go)(haven't experienced)

13 Dialogues in Nepal

BOUDHANATH AND SWAYAMBUNATH

Those of you planning to visit Tibetan communities in Nepal and India will find the phrases introduced in this book applicable—though their focus is on Tibet. We didn't include travel sections that take place in Nepal or India because in those situations communication would occur in Nepali, Hindi, or English.

The following dialogues take place in Nepal, at two of the most revered places by Tibetans. Boudhanath is located a few miles east of Kathmandu, and Swayambunath is just west, high on a hill overlooking the city. We recommend that you visit these places often—perhaps rent a room there—go to the bazaars, talk to pilgrims, explore tea-stalls and *chahng* houses. You'll have lots of opportunities to practice your language skills in these settings.

Stupas (see RELIGIOUS AND MONASTIC VOCABULARY appendix) are the focal points at both of these sacred places. The construction of the Boudha *stupa*, called *Jah-rung kah-shor*, or *Chorten chen-po* ("Great *Stupa*"), was supposedly planned by a devout Tibetan Buddhist woman who received the Nepali king's permission to do so. Throngs of pilgrims, some from the exotic-most reaches of the Tibetan plateau, gather here during the winter months.

Swayambunath (*Phag-pa shing-gun*: self-manifested hill of sublime trees) is also an important place of pilgrimage. The saint Nāgārjuna is said to have scattered his hair on the hill on which sits the *stupa*, and from each hair a tree of a different type grew. Early morning fog, huge statues, deep forests, and monasteries perched high on the hill make this a magical place to visit.

BOUDHANATH DIALOGUE

—This is a sacred place.
   Sah-cha di tsa-chen-po ray
   (place)(this)(important)(is)

—Many pilgrims come here.
   Neh-kor-ken mahng-bo dhey yong-gi-ray
   (pilgrims)   (many)   (here)(come)(are)

—When do most people circumambulate (the *stupa*)?
   Mi mahng-che ko-rah kah-dü gyahp-gi-ray
   (people)(generally)(circle) (when) (doing)
You can also begin your sentences with *mahng-che*. This would mean: "Generally. . ." (followed by whatever you want to state).

—In the morning and evening.
   Sho-gey thang gong-mo la
   (morning)(and)(evening)(in)

—Around the *stupa* are many stores.
   Chor-ten gi tha-kor la tsong-khang mahng-bo yo-ray
   (*stupa*)   (around) (at) (store)   (many)   (are)

—Are there many monasteries here?
   Dhey gom-pa mahng-bo yo-ray-peh
   (here)(monastery)(many) (are there)

—There are many monasteries of different sects.
   Chö-luk mahng-bo gi gom-pa yo-ray
   (sect)   (many)   (of)(monastery)(are)

—Where are they? Please show me.
   Kah-bah yo-ray? Ngah la teh-ro-nahng
   (where) (are)   (me) (to)(show)(please)

—The large one there is Nyingma.
   Chen-po pha-ghey Nying-ma ray
   (big)   (there)   "   (is)

—This one is Gelug.
  Di Geh-lug ray
  (this) " (is)

—What's that big red one up the road?
  Mahr-po chen-po pha-ghey kah-gi ray
  (red) (big) (that) (which) (is)

—That one is Sakya.
  Pha-ghey Sah-kya ray
  (that) " (is)

—Do all the sects have monasteries here?
  Chö-luk tsahng-ma gi gom-pa dhey yo-ray-peh
  (sect) (all) (of)(monastery)(here)(have)

—Do many westerners live here?
  In-jee mahng-bo dhey deh-gi-ray-peh
  (western)(many) (here)(stay)(are)

—Are rooms available around here?
  Dhey khang-mi rah-gi-ray-peh
  (here)(room) (obtain)(will)

—Sometimes.
  Kahp kahp-la

—In winter it's difficult to find vacant rooms.
  Gun-gah, khang-mi thong-ba rah-yah kah-leh kah-po ray
  (winter) (room) (empty) (to get) (difficult) (is)

—You have to ask around.
  Keh-cha tri-goh-ray
  (ask)(question)(need)

—Do any lamas speak English?
  In-jee-keh gyahp-ken la-ma yo-ray-peh
  (English) (speaking) " (are there)

—Can I go onto the *stupa*?
  Chor-ten gi gahng-la dro cho-gi-ray-peh
  (*stupa*) (of) (on) (go) (is it allowed)

SWAYAMBUNATH DIALOGUE

—Where is the Swayambu *stupa*?
Phag-pa shing-gun gi chor-ten kah-bah yo-ray
(Swayambunath) (of)(*stupa*) (where) (is)

—It is at the top of the hill.
Ree pha-ghey gahng-la yo-ray
(hill) (there) (on top) (is)

—How do you get there?
Pha-ghey kahn-dre-si dro-goh-ray
(there) (how) (go) (need)

—You have to climb these stairs.
Ken-zah din-tso zah-goh-ray
(stairs) (these) (climb)(need)

—There are so many stairs!
Ken-zah mahng-bo shi-tah du!
(stairs) (many) (very) (are)

—Go slowly.
Kah-leh la gyu
(slowly) (go)

—From the top you will see the whole city (of Kathmandu).
Tse-neh,   gyah-sah tsahng-ma thong-gi-ray
(from top), (city) (all) (see) (will)

—What's that large gold thing?
Chen-po, ser-po pha-ghey kah-rey ray
(big) (yellow) (that) (what) (is)

—That is a *vajra*.   (see RELIGIOUS AND MONASTIC
Pha-ghey dor-jeh ray   VOCABULARY for an
(that) (dorje) (is)   explanation)

—Are there monasteries here?
Dhey gom-pa yo-ray-peh
(here)(monastery)(are there)

—There are several.
Kah-shey yo-ray
(several) (are)

—Where are they?
Kah-bah yo-ray
(where) (are)

—Some are near the *stupa*.
Kah-shey chor-ten gi thi-la yo-ray
(several) (*stupa*) (near)(to) (are)

—Other monasteries are down below.
Gom-pa shen-dah woh-la yo-ray
(monastery)(other)(below) (are)

—May I go inside the monastery?
Ngah gom-pa nahng la dro cho-gi-ray-peh
(I) (monastery) (in) (to)(go) (is it allowed)

—If the doors are open, it's okay.
Go che yö-nah, di-gi-ray
(door)(open)(if), (it is okay)

—Where does that road go?
Lahm-kah di kah-bah dro-gi-ray
(road) (this)(where)(goes)

—That road encircles (Swayambu) hill.
Lahm-kah pha-ghey ree kor-gi-yo-ray
(road) (that) (hill)(around)(does)

—People circumambulate this hill on that road.
Mi-tso lahm-kah di la ree ko-rah gyahp-gi-yo-ray
(people) (road) (this) (hill)(circumambulate)

—How long does it take?
Ko-rah gyahp-yah la gyu-ring-lö goh-gi-ray
(circumambulate)(to)(time)(how long)(need)

—About 45 minutes.
Kar-ma shi-chu sha-ngah tsah
(minutes)   (45)   (about)

—Are there nunneries near Swayambunath?
Phag-pa shing-gun gi thi-la ah-ni gom-pa yo-ray-peh
(Swayambunath) (near)   (nun)(monastery)(are there)

—One is near Ring Road.   (Ring Road encircles the entire
Chik Ring Road gi thi-la yo-ray   city of Kathmandu and
(one) ”   ”   (near) (is)   passes Swayambunath at
                                            one point)

14 Transportation

VOCABULARY

by walking: **khom-ba gyahp neh**
by car: **mo-tah la**
by bus: **lahm-khor la**
by bicycle: **kahng-gah-ri la**
by airplane: **nahm-dru la**

north: **chahng**
south: **lo**
east: **shahr**
west: **noop**

far distance: **tha ring-bo**
short distance: **tha nye-bo**
direction: **chok**
in front of: **tsa la**
behind: **gyahp la**
right: **yeh-ba**
left: **yön-ba**
up/go up: **yah/zah (climb)**
down/go down: **mah/mah pahp**
straight: **kah-too**
opposite side: **pha-cho**
next to: **(gi) thi la**

1) From _____ to _____.
      Lhasa   Shigatse

    _____ neh _____ phar-tu
    Lhasa   **Shi-gah-tse**

2) Where is _____?
    a bicycle for rent
    the bus to Lhasa
    the bus to Shigatse

    _____ kah-bah yo-ray
    kahng-gah-ri la-cha la
    Lhasa dro-ken lahm-khor
    Shi-gah-tse dro-ken
                 lahm-khor

3) Will you take me to ____?
    Ngah la _____ **la tree-geh**
    (I)   (to)(take)(will)

4) Is this the bus to ____?   ____ **la dro-ken lahm-khor**
                                          (to) (going) (bus)
                                     di ray-peh
                                        (this)(is it)

5) I want to go to ____.   **Ngah** ____ **la dron-do-yö**
                                (I)   (to) (go) (want)

6) I need to go to ____.   **Ngah** ____ **la dro-goh-yö**
                                (I)   (to) (go) (need)

7) From _____ to _____ how far is it?
   _____ **neh** _____ **phar-tu tha ring-lö yo-ray**
        (from)   (between)(distance)(long)(how)(is it)

8) From _____ to _____ how long does it take?
   _____**neh** _____ **phar-tu chu-tsö kah-tsö goh-gi-ray**
        (from)   (between)(time)(how much)(need)

9) From Lhasa to Shigatse I will go by bus.
   Ngah Lhasa neh Shi-gah-tse phar-tu lahm-khor la dro-gi-yin
   (I)   ''   (from)   ''   (between)   (bus)   (by)
   (go)(will)

10) Can we stop here?
    Dhey kahk cho-gi-ray-peh
    (here)(stop)(is it allowed)

11) Please stop/Please wait   (or)   Wait a moment.
    Kahk-nahng / Gu-nahng   (or)   **De-tsi gu ah**
For stronger commands drop the tense ending and say the verb
root. See COMMANDS section for more information.

12) I want to get off.
    Ngah phap-gi-yin
    (I)(going down)(am)

13) What time are we ____?   **Ngah-tso chu-tsö kah-tsö**
                                              la ____ **ray**
                leaving   **dro-ya**

arriving	**lep-ya**
stopping	**kahk-ya**

14) Tell me when we reach _____.
    Ngah-tso _____ lep-dü, ngah-la lahp-ro-nahng
    (we)   (arrive)(when)(to me)(tell)(please)
    The verb root + *dü* means "when (the verb) happens...". So
    ngah-tso lep-dü means "when we arrive...".

15) Are you going or staying?
    Keh-rahng dro-geh, deh-geh
    (you)   (going), (staying)

16) I have a small/big load.
    Ngah la toh-bo choong choong/ chen-po yö
    (I)   (to)(load)   (small) / (big)(have)

17) Which is the way to Lhasa?
    Lhasa gi lahm-kah kah-gi ray
       '' (of)(road)   (which)(is)

18) Where does this road go?
    Lahm-kah di kah-bah dro-gi-ray
    (road)   (this)(where)(goes)

19) Is accommodation available on the road?
    Lahm-kah la deh-sah rah-gi-ray-peh
    (road)   (on)(place to stay)(obtain)(will)

SHORT DISTANCE TRAVEL

Though cardinal and intermediate directions are given in some
of the dialogues, they really aren't used much. Tibetans will just
point out a direction, or tell you to follow a particular road for
a certain length of time.

They calculate distance in terms of time. This can be "walking time" or "driving time". Often it's easier to catch a ride on
an outgoing truck or bus than to walk or bicycle to sites around
Lhasa. However, some truck drivers these days are concerned
about losing their driving permits should they pick up western-

ers, as this has supposedly occured in the recent past. In Nepal, bicycles are handy, as are three-wheeled scooters and taxis.

Should you decide to swim somewhere, say in the Lhasa River, it's best to wear an Indian *lungi* (a lightweight cotton wrap). They wrap high above the chest on a woman and hang down to the knees. A man can wrap his around the waist.

SHORT DISTANCE DIALOGUES

—Where are you going?   (you say to the driver)
  Keh-rahng kah-bah dro-geh
  (you)   (where) (going)

—We're going to Nyingchi (he says to you).
  Ngah-tso Nyingchi la dro-gi-yin
  (we)   ”   (to) (going)

—Where is that?
  Kah-bah ray
  (where)   (is)

—Beyond Tsedang.
  Tsedang gi jeh-la
       ”   (beyond)

—I'm also going to Tsedang.
  Ngah yeh Tsedang la dro-gi-yin
  (I)   (also)   ”   (to) (going)(am)

—Can I come with you?
  Ngah keh-rahng nyem-do yong-nah di-gi-ray-peh
  (I)   (you)   (with)   (come)(if) (is it alright)

—Okay get in back.
  Di-gi-ray, gyahp-la shön
  (okay)   (back) (in)(ride)

—May I sit in the cab?
  Lahm-khor gi dün-la deh-nah di-gi-ray-peh
  (vehicle) (in front) (sit)(if) (is it okay)

—You cannot go with us.

Keh-rahng ngah-tso nyem-do dro cho-gi-mah-ray
(you)   (us)   (with)   (go)   (not allowed)

—Why?

Kah-rey che-neh

—We lose our driving permit if we pick up westerners.

In-jee mo-tah la kye-nah, ngah-tsö mo-tah gi lah-kyer
(westerners)(auto)(in)(bring)(if), (we) (auto) (of) (permit)
thoh-gi-ray
(confiscate)

TSEDANG

This is a town located southeast of Lhasa in the Yarlung River
Valley. Sitting at an elevation of over two miles, Tsedang is situ-
ated amidst barley fields and sites important to the development
of Tibetan civilization. Just east of Tsedang, in a sacred mountain, lies the cave where two deities who incarnated as a monkey
and ogress gave birth to the Tibetan people.

—Where is the bazaar?

Trom kah-bah yo-ray
(market)(where)(is)

—Turn right here. It's just up ahead.

Di neh yeh-ba gyu. Yah, cha yo-ray
(from here)(right)(go). (up) (just)(is)

—Many traders go to this bazaar.

Phö-beh tsong-pa mahng-bo trom di la dro-gi-ray
(Tibetan)(traders) (many) (bazaar)(this)(to) (go)

—Are there important places to visit around here?

Di-ba-la (accent middle syllable) **sah-cha tsa-chen-po**
(around here)   (places)   (powerful)
yo-ray-peh
(are there)

—Yes. One is behind the hospital.

Yo ray. Chik men-khang gi gyahp-lo-la yo-ray
(yes)   (one)   (hospital)   (behind)   (is)

This is where the first cultivated field in Tibet was planted by the monkey deity mentioned above.

—Where is this hospital?
Men-khang di kah-bah yo-ray
(hospital) (this)(where) (is)

—Go up this road and then turn left.
Lahm-kah di la yah gyu, a-ni yön-ba gyu
(road) (this) (up) (go), (and)(left) (go)

—How do I get to the Yumbu Monastery?
Yum-bu lha-khang la kahn-dre-si dro-goh-ray
  "   (temple) (to) (how)   (go)(need)

—It is about one hour from Nedong if you walk.
Neh-dong neh khom-ba gyahp-nah chu-tsö chik ray
  "   (from)   (walk)   (if) (hour) (one)(is)

—Otherwise if you get on the road early you can catch a ride.
Yah-meh-na, lahm-kah la ngah-bo deh-nah, mo-tah rah-gi-ray
(otherwise) (road) (to) (early) (stay)(if) (auto) (get)(will)

—The other way (from Nedong) goes to Chonggyai.
Shahr-chok gi lahm-kah Chong-gye la dro-gi-ray
(eastern)   (road)   "   (to) (goes)

—How far is Chonggyai?
Chong-gye tha ring-lö yo-ray
  "   (distance)(how far)(is)

—About half an hour.
Chu-tsö che-kah tsah
(hour) (half) (about)

—Near the bridge is a powerful place.   (This is the burial
Sahm-pa gi thi-la sah-cha tsa-chen-po yo-ray   site for
(bridge) (near) (place) (important) (is)   many famous
                                        Tibetan kings)
—I understand. Thank you.
Ngey ha-kho-song. Thu-chi che
(I)   (understand). (thank you)

SAMYE BY TRUCK

Samye was the first monastery built in Tibet. It was founded by Padmasambhava (Guru Rinpoche), the progenitor of Buddhism in Tibet, in the eighth century. Located in the Yarlung Valley, west of Tsedang, Samye is accessible from the south, only by ferry. It was here that the great debate occurred between a Chinese Buddhist practitioner and an Indian one. As the latter was considered victorious, Indian rather than Chinese Buddhism was chosen as the model from which Tibetan Buddhism evolved.

GOING TO SAMYE BY TRUCK DIALOGUE

—I'm going to Samye.
   Ngah Sahm-yeh la dro-gi-yin
   (I)   "   (to)(going)

—Go and get in back, then.
   Gyahp-la shön
   (back)(in)(ride)

—Let me off at the ferry.
   Ngah la thu-chung la kye-ro-nahng
   (me) (to) (ferry) (to) (take)(please)

—What time does the ferry leave?
   Thu-chung chu-tsö kah-tsö la dro-gi-ray
   (ferry)   (time) (how much)(at)(go)(will)

—(The next one is) at noon. The following one is at three.
   Nying-ku la. Di gi jeh-la chik chu-tsö sum la dro-gi-ray
   (noon)(at). (this)(after) (one) (hour)   (3) (at) (go)(will)

—There is a lot of dust on the road today.
   Lahm-kah la thi-ring teh-lah mahng-bo du
   (road)   (on) (today) (dust) (much)   (is)

—Cover your face with your scarf.
   Kah-ti gi dong-ba kahp-nahng
   (scarf) (face) (cover)(please)

Having the *ro* particle removed from the command creates a less polite, and more informal effect.

—The sun is very hot today.
Thi-ring nyi-ma tsah-po shi-tah du
(today) (sun) (hot) (very) (is)

—Put on your hat.
Shah-mo khön-nahng
(hat) (wear)(please)

—The truck is going slow/ too fast, I'm scared!
Lahm-khor kah-leh la dro-gi-du / gyo-tahk gi-du, Ngah
(truck) (slow) (goes) / (too fast) (goes), (I)
sheh-gi-du!
(scared)(am)

—We're at the ferry! Give me Y5 for the ride.
Thu-chong la lep-song! Ngah la quai ngah teh-ro-nahng
(ferry) (arrived) (to me) (coin) (5) (give)(please)

—No, people in back ride for free.
Teh-gi-meh, gyahp-la shön-nah teh-goh-mah-ray
(give) (not), (back)(at) (ride)(if) (give)(need)(not)

—(to the ferryman) Take me to Samye.
Sahm-yeh la kye-ro-nahng
(Samye) (to)(take)(please)

—That's a wonderful place. Padmasambhava built it.
Sah-cha peh kyi-bo du. Guru Rin-po-chay gi sö-pah-ray
(place)(very)(pleasant)(is). " (build)(did)

—How many monks live there now?
Tra-pa kah-tsö pha-ghey deh-gi-yo-ray
(monks)(how many)(there)(staying)
You might use the honorific form of "stay" here: *shoo*

—About thirty.
Sum-chu tsah
(30) (about)

—Please show me the main hall and the chanting hall.
  Ngah la chok-chen thang thön-khang teh-ro-nahng
  (to me) (main hall) (and) (chanting hall)(show)(please)

—Follow me, they are over there.
  Ngey shoog-la phe, pha-ghey yo-ray
  (me)   (after)(come), (there)(are)

—The center of the temple is the center of the world.
  Lha-khang gi kyi, zahm-bu-ling gi kyi ray
  (temple)(this)(middle), (world)(middle)(is)

—I don't understand.
  Ha-kho-mah-song

—The center of the temple and the center of the world are the same.
  Lha-khang gi kyi a-ni zahm-bu-ling gi kyi chik-ba ray
  (temple) (of)(middle)(and) (world) (of)(middle)(same)(are)

—There is no difference.
  Kye-ba yo-mah-ray
  (difference)(have)(not)

—Where do the monks assemble?
  Tra-pa-tso chok-sah kah-bah yo-ray
  (monks) (meet)(place)(where)(is)

—Over there.
  Pha-ghey yo-ray
  (there) (is)

—There are five statues on the altar here.
  Chö-shum la ku ngah du
  (altar)   (on)(statues) (5) (are)

—The one in the middle is Padmasambhava.
  Kyi gi di Guru Rin-po-chay ray
  (middle)(that)   "   (is)

—I heard that in the south chapel there is an important Avalokiteshwara statue

(Deity of Compassion, as mentioned earlier).

Gom-pa gi lho-chok la chen-reh-zi gi ku tsa-chen-po chik
(monastery) (south) (at) '' (of)(statue)(powerful)(one)
yo-ray, ngey koh-song
(is) (I) (heard)

Again the use of "I heard". Remember, everything that precedes *ngey koh-song* is what was heard.

—You can see everything from the roof.

Tho-ga neh tsahng-ma thong-gi-ray
(roof) (from) (all) (see) (will)

LONG DISTANCE TRAVEL

Travel guidebooks and local information can supply you with help on this subject. Usually westerners pay double the local rate on busses and are told to sit in the back (who else would sit back there?). Try using your Tibetan phrases to get both local rates and treatment on busses. International Student Identification Cards also can help. Applications can be obtained from Council Information Educational Exchange offices found in major cities.

Sometimes on a pilgrim bus you, as passengers, can decide among yourselves where to detour on the way to your final destination. This may involve an additional amount of money to be paid to the driver.

When the bus stops it is best to know for how long, why, and by whose watch time decisions are made. Make sure you synchronize your watch with that person's. Some travelers may be on Beijing time while others are on Lhasa time. Don't forget a scarf for the dusty roads and a hat and dark glasses for the sun.

LONG DISTANCE TRUCKING DIALOGUE

—I want to go to Lhasa.

Ngah Lhasa la dron-dö-yö
(I) '' (to) (go)(want)

—Come with us (on a pilgrim bus).
  Ngah-tso nyem-do sho
  (us)   (with)   (come)
Sho is the command for "come". See the COMMANDS section.

—Are you going directly to Lhasa?
  Keh-rahng Lhasa la kah-too dro-gi-yin-peh
  (you)   "   (to)(directly)(going)(are)

—Maybe we'll also go to Sakya on the way.
  Chik che-nah ngah-tsö Sah-kya la yeh dro-gi-yin
  (maybe)   (we)   "   (to)(also)(go)(will)

—How much more do we have to pay (to go to Sakya)?
  Tho-ba ngü kah-tsö teh-goh-ray
  (extra)(money)(how much)(give)(need)

—If we each pay Y3, we can stop in Sakya.
  Ngah-tso quai sum sum teh-nah, Sah-kya la mo-tah
  (we)   (coin) (3) (3) (give)(if)   "   (to) (auto)
kahk-gi-ray
(stop)(will)

—I will pay.
  Ngah teh-gi-yin
  (I)   (give)(will)

—(driver): You must pay me Y60 and sit in back.
  Keh-rahng quai trook-chu teh, a-ni gyahp-la deh-goh-ray
  (you)   (coin) (60)   (give)(and)(back) (at)(sit)(need)

—Tibetans don't pay more than Y30.
  Phö-beh mi quai sum-chu leh teh-gi-min-du
  (Tibetan)(people)(coin)(30)(compare)(give)(not)

—Westerners must pay more and sit in back.
  In-jee-tso ngü mahng-wa teh-goh-ray, a-ni gyahp-la
  (westeners)(money)(more) (give)(need) (and)(back)(at)
deh-goh-ray
(sit)

—I have a Student Identification Card.
Ngah la lop-trook gi lah-kyer yö
(I)   (student)(of)(permit)(have)

The word *lah-kyer* can be used for any type of permit: passport, visa, innoculation record, and so on.

—Okay, then give me Y30 please.
Lah-so, di yin-nah quai sum-chu teh-nahng
(okay),(in that case)(coin)(30)   (give)(please)

—We're stopping here now.
Than-dah ngah-tso dhey kahk-gi-yin
(now)   (we)   (here) (stop)(will)

—Will we spend the entire night here?
Ngah-tso dhey tsen-kahng deh-ya ray-peh
(we)   (here) (night) (all)(staying)(are)

—No, just five hours.
Mah-ray, chu-tsö ngah chik-po
(no),   (hour) (5) (only)

—We will leave at three in the morning.
Ngah-tso sahng-nyi sho-gey, chu-tsö sum-ba la dro-gi-yin
(we)   (tomorrow)(morning), (hour) (3)   (at)(go)(will)

—Who has Lhasa time?
Lhasa gi chu-tsö su la yö
    "   (of) (time)(who)(has)

—Go look at the driver's watch.
Mo-tah tahng-ken gi chu-tsö la tah
(auto) (driver)   (of)(watch)(at)(look)

—What time is it?
Chu-tsö kah-tsö ray
(time) (how much)(is)

—It's ten o'clock.
Chu-tsö chu-ba ray
(hour)   (10) (is)

The word *chu-tsö* is used for "watch," "clock," "hour," and "o'clock." See NUMBERS and TIME in the back for more information.

—Why are we stopping here?
Ngah-tso dhey kah-rey che-neh kahk-pah-ray
(we)   (here)   (why)   (stopped)

—How long are we stopping here?
Ngah-tso dhey gyu-ring-lö kahk-ya ray
(we)   (here)(time)(how long)(stopping)(are)
There is a difference between *gyu-ring-lö* and *tha-ring-lö*. *Tha* refers to distance and *gyu* to time. One is "for how long a time?" and the other "for how long a distance?"
   The sentence above can also be said like this:
Ngah-tso thu-tsö kah-tsö kahk-ya ray
(we)   (time)(how much)(stopping)(are)

—Is food available in this village?
Trong-sehp di la kah-lah rah-gi-ray-peh
(village)   (this)(at)(food)   (obtain)(will)

—I'm not going further with you.
Ngah keh-rahng nyem-do dro-gi-meh
(I)   (you)   (with)   (going)(not)

—I want to stay here for a few days.
Dhey nyi-ma kah-shey deh-gi-yin
(here)(day)   (several)   (staying)

15 Visiting a Tibetan Doctor

Tibetan medicine is effective in curing a number of ailments, especially internal disorders. Don't hesitate to visit Tibetan doctors if you are unwell. Their methods of diagnosis include the taking of pulses in the wrist, examining the eyes, and checking the urine. After a diagnosis is made, you are usually sent to an adjoining room where the medicine is dispensed.

This medicine is in the form of pills, made from a variety of crushed ingredients depending on the illness they are to cure. You are usually given two or three different kinds to take. The doctors will designate which pills are to be taken when and the method of consumption. If you are unsure, have them write the diagnosis on a piece of paper and have someone translate it for you.

blood: **trahk**

body: **sug-po**

cough: **lo** (lo gyahp: verb)

cut/sore: **mah**

disease: **nah-tsa**

ear: **ahm-jo**

fever: **tsah-wa**

mouth: **kha**

pill: **ri-pu**

pulse: **tsa**

stool: **kyahk-pa**

tongue: **chay**

urine: **chin-ba**

medicine: **men**

medicine for headaches:

go men

eye ointment: **mik men**

cough medicine: **lo men**

1)   Where is a _____?   _____ **kah-bah yo-ray**
   a) western doctor   a) **in-jee ahm-jee**
   b) Tibetan doctor   b) **Phö-beh ahm-jee**
   c) hospital   c) **men-khang**
   d) pharmacy   d) **men tsong-khang**

2)   My _____ hurts.   **Ngey** ____ **nah-gi-du**
   a) eye   a) **mik**
   b) head   b) **go**
   c) stomach   c) **tro-go**
   d) tooth   d) **soh**
   e) leg   e) **kahng-ba**
   f) hand/arm   f) **lahk-ba**
   g) throat   g) **mik-ba**
   h) chest   h) **pahng-ko**

3)   I have _____.   **Ngah la** _____ **yö**
   a) a sore   a) **mah (chik)**
   b) a fever   b) **tsah-wa**

4)   I have _____.   **Ngah** ____ **gi-du**
   a) a cough   a) **lo gyahp-**
   b) diarrhoea   b) **tro-ko sheh-**

5)   I feel _____.   **Ngah** _____ **gi-du**
   a) sick   a) **nah-**
   b) dizzy   b) **go-yoo kor-**
   c) nauseous   c) **kyuk-meh lahng-**

6)   Take this ____ a day.   **Nyi-ma chik la**_____
                                            sah-goh-ray
   a) once   a) **theng chik**
   b) twice   b) **theng nyi**

7)   Each time take ____   **Theng ray ray ri-pu**
                    pill/pills.   ____ **sah**
   a) one   a) **chik**
   b) two   b) **nyi**

8)   For _____ days.   **Nyi-ma ____ phar-tu**
                                              (or) **la**

    a) eight   a) **geh**
    b) fifteen   b) **chu-ngah**

9)   Take this pill ____.   **Ri-pu di ____ sah**
    a) in the morning   a) **sho-gey**
    b) in the afternoon   b) **nying-ku**
    c) in the evening   c) **gong-mo**
    d) at night   d) **tsen la**

    e) before eating   e) **kah-lah mah-seh khong-la**
    f) after eating   f) **kah-lah seh-neh**

    g) with your food   g) **kah-lah nyem-do**
    h) with hot water   h) **chu tsah-po nyem-do**
    i) with tea   i) **cha nyem-do**
    j) with milk   j) **o-mah nyem-do**

Note the phrase "before eating". The form is noun + negative + verb + *khong la*. This means "before (the verb)...".

10) Please call a doctor.
Ahm-jee keh tahng-ro-nahng
(doctor) (call) (please)

11) Do you have medicine?
Keh-rahng la men yö-peh
(you) (to)(medicine)(have)

12) Please buy this medicine for me.
Ngah la men di nyo-ro-nahng
(for me)(medicine)(this)(buy)(please)

13) Give me some water.
Ngah la chu teh
(me)(to)(water)(give)

14) I will lie down.
Ngah mah nyeh-gi-yin
(I)(down)(lay)(will)

15) I have been sick for several days.

Ngah nah-neh nyi-ma kah-shey chin-song

(I) (sick)(since)(day)(several)(has gone)

The verb root + *neh* means "since (the verb)...". In this case, "Since I was sick...".

TIBETAN MEDICINE DIALOGUE

—I want to see a Tibetan doctor.

Ngah Phö-beh ahm-jee jeh-goh-yö

(I) (Tibetan)(doctor) (meet)(need)

Jeh is the honorific form of *toop*, the verb for "meet".

—The Tibetan hospital is near the Jokhang.

Phö-beh men-khang Jo-khang gi thi-la yo-ray

(Tibetan)(hospital)   "   (near) (is)

—The doctors there are skillful.

Pha-ghey ahm-jee khey-bo shi-tah yo-ray

(there) (doctors) (skillful) (very) (are)

—One speaks some English.

Chik in-jee-keh de-tsi shing-gi-ray

(one)(English) (a little) (know)(does)

—Will you go with me please?

Keh-rahng ngah nyem-do yong-gi-yin-peh

(you)   (I) (with)   (come) (will)

—Is it open now?

Than-dah go che-yo-ray-peh

(now)   (door)(open)(is)

—Hello, what's wrong with you?

Tah-shi de-leh, kah-rey nah-gi-du

(greetings),   (what) (hurt)(does)

—I don't feel well / my throat hurts / my stomach is upset.

Ngah de-bo min-du / ngey mik-pa nah-gi-du / ngey tro-go

(I) (well) (not) / (my) (throat) (hurts) / (my)(stomach)

nah-gi-du

(upset)(is)

—It seems like my finger is broken.
Ngey zoo-gu chahk-pa nahng-shin du
(my)(finger) (broken) (just like)(is)

—Please sit down.
Dhey shoo-ro-nahng
(here)(sit)(please)

—Where?
Kah-bah

—Many people are waiting, go wait with them.
Mi mahng-bo gu du, khon-tsö nyem-do gu-ro-nahng
(people)(many)(wait)(are), (they) (with) (wait)(please)

—(to person sitting next to you) What happened?
Kah-rey che-song

—I have a sore.
Ngah la mah yö
(I)   (sore)(have)

—Show the doctor well.
Ahm-jee la yahk-po teh-ro-nahng
(doctor)(to)(well) (show)(please)

(This is commonly said to someone on their way to see the doctor. It's difficult to translate)

—(with the doctor) Sit still.
Tsu-gu deh
(still) (sit)

—What are you doing?
Kah-rey che-gi-yö
(what) (doing)(are)

—I'm feeling your pulse.
Keh-rahng gi tsa tah-gi-yö
(your)   (pulse) (looking)(am)

—I'm looking at your eyes (for diagnosis).
Ngah keh-rahng gi mik tah-gi-yö
(I)   (your)   (eyes) (look)(am)

—I need to check your urine.
Ngah keh-rahng gi chin-ba tah-goh-yö
(I)   (your)   (urine) (look)(need)

—Please pee in this cup.

Kah-yul di la chin-ba tahng-ro-nahng

(cup) (this)(in) (urinate) (please)

—The problem is that the vital air is blocked here.

Keh-rahng gi lung dhey gah-du

(your) (inner air)(here)(blocked)

According to the Tibetan system of medicine (as with Acupuncture, Shiatsu and other oriental systems of healing), a healthy body is the result of subtle airs or meridians within the body being in balance. When there is a blockage, the Tibetan doctor may say that these inner airs have stopped.

—It is serious/ not serious.

Nyen-kah-chen-po ray / nyen-kah-chen-po mah-ray

(danger) (great) (is) / (danger) (great) (is not)

—Please write the name of the problem on this piece of paper.

Nah-tsah gi ming shu-gu di la thi-ro-nahng

(disease) (of)(name)(paper)(this)(write)(please)

—Will you write it in English?

In-jee-yigi la thi-geh

(English) (write)(will)

Geh is the shortened version of *gi-yin-peh* as explained in the grammar section.

—Take this paper to that other room.

Shu-gu di khang-mi shen-dah la kye-nahng

(paper)(this)(room) (other) (to)(take)(please)

—(You) will receive the medicine there.

Pha-ghey men rah-gi-ray

(there)(medicine)(obtain)(will)

—Hello, let me see the piece of paper.

Tah-shi de-leh, shu-gu ngah la teh-ro-nahng

(hello) , (paper) (to me) (show)(please)

—One moment, I'll get the pills.

Gu nahng (or) **kar-ma chik, ngah ri-pu len-gi-yin**

(wait)(please) or (minute)(one),(I) (pill) (bring)(will)

—What do I do with these?

Ngah din-tso nyem-do kah-rey che-goh-ray
(I)   (these)   (with)   (what)   (do)(need)

—Take these pills in the morning.

Ri-pu din-tso sho-gey sah-nahng
(pills)(these) (morning) (eat)(please)

—Take these others at noon, and these with dinner.

Shen-dah nying-ku la, a-ni din-tso gong-mo kah-lah nyem-do sah
(other) (noon) (at), (and) (these) (dinner) (food) (with) (eat)

The use of the verb without *ro-nahng* or *nahng* is a more powerful command. However in this case it is an informal use rather than a harsh one.

—Take them on an empty stomach/ with food.

Tro-go thong-ba la sah-nahng / kah-lah nyem-do sah-nahng
(stomach)(empty)(on)(eat)(please)/(food)(with) (eat)(please)

—First chew them and then drink warm water.

Tahng-bo so-gyahp, deh-neh chu tsah-po nyem-do sah-nahng
(first)   (chew), (and then) (water)(hot) (with) (eat)(please)

—I understand. Thank you.

Ngey ha-kho-song. Thu-chi che
(I) (understand).   (thank you)

—How much do I owe?

Ngü kah-tsö ray
(money)(how much)(is)

—Y5 please.

Quai ngah teh-ro-nahng
(coin)(5) (give)(please)

PART THREE

APPENDICES

16 Numbers

Numbers are easy to learn since 1 through 10 repeat themselves throughout the system. Prefixes attached to these numbers do vary, however. The first horizontal column lists numbers from 1 to 10. Beyond 10, add the appropriate prefix from the vertical column on the far left. When a number is exact, say 10, 20 or 100, the suffix *tahm-ba* is added. The column on the far right lists these vertically.

	chik(1)	nyi(2)	sum(3)	shi(4)	ngah(5)	trook(6)	diin(7)	geh(8)	gu(9)	chu (10)
chu +	" (11)	" (12)	" (13)	" (14)	" (15)	" (16)	" (17)	" (18)	" (19)	nyi-shu tahm-bah (20)
nyi-shu tsah +	" (21)	" (22)	" (23)	" (24)	" (25)	" (26)	" (27)	" (28)	" (29)	sum-chu , (30)
sum-chu so +	" (31)	" (32)	" (33)	" (34)	" (35)	" (36)	" (37)	" (38)	" (39)	shi-chu , (40)
shi-chu sha +	" (41)	" (42)	" (43)	" (44)	" (45)	" (46)	" (47)	" (48)	" (49)	ngah-chu , (50)
ngah-chu ngah +	" (51)	" (52)	" (53)	" (54)	" (55)	" (56)	" (57)	" (58)	" (59)	trook-chu , (60)
trook-chu rah +	" (61)	" (62)	" (63)	" (64)	" (65)	" (66)	" (67)	" (68)	" (69)	diin-chu , (70)
diin-chu dohn +	" (71)	" (72)	" (73)	" (74)	" (75)	" (76)	" (77)	" (78)	" (79)	geh-chu , (80)
geh-chu gyah +	" (81)	" (82)	" (83)	" (84)	" (85)	" (86)	" (87)	" (88)	" (89)	gu-chu , (90)
gu-chu go +	" (91)	" (92)	" (93)	" (94)	" (95)	" (96)	" (97)	" (98)	" (99)	gyah , (100)

nyi-gyah (200), sum-gyah (300) shi-gyah (400) and so on.
chik tong (1000), nyi tong (2000), sum tong (3000), and so on.

17 Time

Phrases for time-related matters include:

1) What time is it?
   Chu-tsö kah-tsö ray
   (hour) (how much)(is)

2) It is 5 o'clock.
   Chu-tsö ngah-ba ray
   (o'clock) (five) (is)

Use the hour plus *ba* to designate an exact hour.

3) It is 5:30.
   Chu-tsö ngah thang che-kah ray
   (o'clock)(five) (and) (half) (is)

Unless the time is on the exact hour, you drop the *ba* suffix. In this case you add *tahng che-kah* meaning half past the hour.

$$\text{hour} + \textit{tahng che-kah} = \text{half past the hour}$$
$$\text{(and) (half)}$$

4) It is 5:20.
   Chu-tsö ngah tahng kar-ma nyi-shu ray
   (o'clock)(five) (and) (minute) (20) (is)

The formula for minutes after the hour:

hour + *tahng kar-ma* + number of minutes = number of
       (and)(minutes)   minutes past
                                             the hour

5) It is 4:40.

Chu-tsö ngah sim-ba-la kar-ma nyi-shu du
(o'clock)(five) (before) (minute) (20)   (is)

For minutes before the hour, use the following hour as reference
(for 4:40 use 5 o'clock) plus *sim-ba-la kar-ma* (before minutes)
and the amount:

hour + *sim-ba-la kar-ma* + number of minutes = number of
       (before) (minutes)   minutes before
                                                  the hour

18 Dates and Days of the Week

Tibetan months are referred to simply as "first month": *dah-wah tahng-bo*, "second month": *dah-wah nyi-ba*, and so on, through the twelfth month: *dah-wah chu-nyi*. The first month of the Tibetan year begins with the New Year (*Loh-sar*), which, since the calendar is based on a lunar system, varies from year to year according to our solar-based one. It usually falls between late January and early March.

The particle that is added to 20's, 30's and so on, as seen previously (NUMBERS), can be dropped when talking about dates.

Tibetan dates are called *tse-ba:*
the 21st: *tse-ba nyi-shu chik* (note the absence of *tsah*)
the 13th: *tse-ba chu-sum*

For the western equivalents you can add the word *in-jee* to the Tibetan words for month and date.

in-jee dah-wah + number, and *in-jee tse-ba* + number

There are at least four important days in the Tibetan month: the new moon (*tse-ba tahng-bo*), the tenth lunar day (*tse-ba chu*), the full moon (*tse-ba chu-ngah*) and the twenty-fifth (*tse-ba nyi-shu ngah*). By following the Tibetan calendar you will know when these and other auspicious days are coming and can plan a trip to a monastery on one of them. You will most likely find some type of monastic ceremony occuring on each of the four days mentioned above.

If you decide to follow the Tibetan calendar, you should be aware that sometimes days are doubled or left out, as are months on occasion. This helps to balance out natural tendencies in the lunar year. The best Tibetan calendar that I have seen for westerners is published by the Rigpa Fellowship, and distributed by Snow Lion Publications, PO Box 6483, Ithaca, New York 14851.

DAYS OF THE WEEK

Monday: **sah dah-wah**
Tuesday: **sah mik-mah**
Wednesday: **sah lahk-pa**
Thursday: **sah phu-bu**
Friday: **sah pah-sahng**
Saturday: **sah pem-ba**
Sunday: **sah nyi-ma**

SEASONS

summer: **yar-gah**
fall: **tön-kah**
winter: **gun-gah**
spring: **chi-kah**

19 Festivals

Tibetan Months

1st month: 1st-7th days—New Year Festival: **Loh-sar**

1st month: 15th day—Butter Lamp Festival: **Chu-ngah chö-pa**

2nd month: 28-29th days—Cleansing negativities: **Gyu-tor**

4th month: this entire month is considered auspicious and is known as **Sa-ga dah-wah**. It is the month of the Buddha's birthday, enlightenment, and death. The effects of actions performed during this time, whether positive or negative, are said to be multiplied many times.

4th month: 7th day—Birth of the Buddha

4th month: 15th day—Buddha's Enlightment/animals are freed: **Sahng-gye du-chen**

4th or 5th month: (July 6)—Dalai Lama's Birthday: **Trun-kar du-chen**

5th month: 14th-16th days—Hanging of Tashilhunpo Thang-ka: **Jam-pay mu-lahm**

5th month: 15th-24th days—World Incense Offering: **Zam-ling kyi-sahng**

6th month: 4th day—Buddha's First Sermon/ Turning the Wheel of the Teachings: **Drug-pa chay sheh** (or) **Chö-khor du-chen**

8th month: 1st-10th days—Horse Racing: **Tha gyur**

9th month: 22nd day—Buddha's descent from Tushita Heaven: **Lha-pahp du-chen**

10th month: 25th day—Tsong Khapa's memorial: **Gahng-den ngahm-jo**

12th month:1st-7th days—Shigatse New Year: **Chang-po Loh-sar**

12th month: 29th day—Cleansing negativities from the year that is ending: **Nyi-shu gu**

USEFUL PHRASES

1) Is there a festival coming up?
   Du-chen chik yong-dö yo-ray-peh
   (festival)(one)(come)(about to)(is there)

2) When is the next festival?
   Di gi jeh-la du-chen kah-dü yo-ray
   (this)(of)(next)(festival)(when) (is)

3) What is this called?
   Du-chen gi ming kah-rey sah
   (festival)(of)(name)(what)(called)

4) During the festival what will happen?
   Du-chen gi kahp-la kah-rey che-gi-ray
   (festival) (time) (at)(what)(happen)(will)
   Or...

   At that time what will happen?
   De-thu kah-rey che-gi-ray
   (at that time)(what)(happen)(will)

20 Helpful Opposites

all:**tsahng-ma**/nothing:**kah-yeh min-du**
beautiful:**zeh-bo**(people) **nying jeh-bo**(objects)/ugly:**doh nye-bo**
before:**ngeh-la**/after:**shoog-la**
better:**yah-gah**/worse:**doo-ga**
big:**chen-po**/small:**choong choong**
broken:**chhak**/fixed:**sö-kyor**
cheap:**keh-bo**/expensive:**kong chen-po**
clean:**tsahng-ma**/dirty:**tsok-pa**
clever:**chahng-bo** (**khey-bo**=skillful)/stupid:**kook-pa**
cold:**trahng-mo**/hot:**tsah-po**
comfortable:**kyi-bo**/uncomfortable:**kyi-bo min-du**
cool:**si-po**/warm:**tro-po**
delicious:**shim-bu**/not tasty:**shim-bu min-du**
different:**kha-gha** (**kye-ba**=difference)/same:**chik-pa**
early:**ngah-bo**/late:**chi-po**
easy:**leh-lah-bo**/hard:**kah-leh kahk-po**
empty:**thong-ba**/full:**kahng**
fast:**gyok-po**/slow:**kah-leh**
fat:**shah gyahk-pa**/skinny:**shah kahm-po**
first:**tahng-bo**/last:**shoog-gu**
good:**yahk-po**/bad:**yahk-po min-du** (or) **duk-cha**
hard:**trahk-po**/soft:**jahm-po**
heavy:**ji-goh**/light:**tsha-bo**
here:**deh**/there:**pha-ghey**

high:**tho-po**/low:**mah-bo**
ill:**nah** (verb)/well:**de-bo** (**trahk**=healed)
important:**keh-chen-po**/unimportant:**keh-chen-po mah-ray**
inside:**nahng-la**/outside:**chi-lo-la**
long:**ring-bo**/short:**thoong thoong**
more:**mahng-ah**/less:**nyoong nyoong**
much:**mahng-bo**/little:**de-tsi**
narrow:**tok-po**/wide:**sheng-ga chen-po**
near:**nye-bo**/far:**tha ring-bo**
now:**than-dah**/then:**deh-neh** (or) **de-thu**
old:**nying-pa**/new:**sar-pa**
old:**gen-go**/young:**lo choong choong**
open:**che**/close:**gyahp**
quiet:**kah kah dhe**(verb)/loud:**keh chen-po**
rare:**kom-po**/common:**zahk-to**
real:**ngu-ney** (**ngo-mah**=authentic)/fake:**zoo-mah**
right:**yeh**/left:**yön**
right:**dig-pa**/wrong:**nor** (verb)
ripe:**mim-pa**/sour:**kyoor-mo** (rotten=**roo-pa**)
sharp:**no-po**/dull:**no-po meh-ba** (blunt)
sour:**kyoor-mo**/sweet:**ngar-mo**
strong:**shook chen-po**/weak:**kyo-po**
thick:**thook-po**/thin:**tha-po**
under:**wo-lah**/over:**gahng-la**
vacant:**thong-ba**/occupied:**thong-ba min-du**
wet:**lom-pa**/dry:**kahm-po**

21 Religious and Monastic Vocabulary

Those words followed by numbers are explained in the next section, EXPLANATIONS TO RELIGIOUS AND MONASTIC VOCABULARY. Italicized words are in Sanskrit.

VERBS

circumambulate: **ko-rah gyahp** (1)
divination: **mo gyahp** (2)
light butter lamps: **chö-may pahr** (3)
light incense: **pö pahr** (3)
meditate: **gom gyahp**
offer: **phul**
perform religious ceremony: **chö-pa phul** (or) **shap-den** (4)
perform religious dance: **chahm** (5)
pray: **mu-lahm gyahp**
prostrate: **cha-tsel** (6)
say *mantra*: **mah-ni dahng**

NOUNS

altar: **chö-shum**
altar bowls: **teeng**
amulet: **gaw**
bell: **tril-bu** (7)
bodhisattva: **chahng-chup sem-pa** (8)

bone: **roo-ko**
butter lamp: **chö-may**
candle: **yahng-la**
ceremonial trumpet: **gyah-ling**
compassion: **nying-jeh**
cymbals: **buk-cha**
Dalai Lama: **Yeh-shi Nor-bu**
deity: **lha/lha-mo** (god/goddess)
faith: **the-pa**
festival: **du-chen**
hermit: **gom-chen**
incense: **pö**
karma (good/bad): **leh** (**yahk-po/yahk-po min-du**)
lama's throne: **shug-ti**
mandala: **kyil-khor** (9)
mantra: **ngahk;mah-ni** (10)
monastery: **gom-pa**
monk: **trah-pa**
mudra: **cha-gya** (11)
nectar: **du-tsi** (12)
nun: **ah-ni**
nunnery: **ah-ni gom-pa**
painting (religious banner): **thang-ka**
pilgrim: **neh-kor-wa**
prayer wheel: **mah-ni kor-lo** (13)
protector: **chö-gyong** (14)
religion (Buddhism): **chö** (or) **nahng-peh chö**
retinue of deity: **soong-meh-khor** (15)
ritual dagger: **phur-ba** (16)
ritual drum (large): **ngah**
ritual hand drum: **dah-ma-ru**
rosary: **treng-ah** (17)
scarf: **kah-tah** (18)
scripture: **peh-cha**
shrine: **lha-khang**
statue: **ku**
stupa: **chor-ten** (19)

teacher and wife: **rin-po-chay** and **sahng-yum** (20)
tutelary deity: **yi-dahm** (21)
vajra: **dor-jeh** (22)

EXPLANATIONS TO RELIGIOUS AND MONASTIC VOCABULARY

1) *circumambulate* (ko-rah gyahp): means to walk around an object. It is customary for Tibetans, as with other cultural groups, to encircle venerated objects or places clockwise. In a monastery or temple, it is disrespectful to walk against this flow—in a counter-clockwise direction. Sometimes even large areas of land are circumambulated, like the five mile-long pilgrims'circuit that once encircled the Potala in Lhasa, or the circuit around Tashil-hunpo Monastery in Shigatse.

When you come to a sacred object—a *stupa*, a lama's throne, an altar, shrine, even a pile of stones—pass it on your right. If you enter a monastery in which a ceremony is being performed, feel free to move about, encircling the main hall clockwise along the periphery. Again, if in doubt follow the example of others.

2) *divination* (mo gyahp): a lama performs this activity on special occasions when an answer to a question is sought. It can be done a number of ways; for instance the lama might throw dice or count out a certain number of beads on his or her rosary. Westerners may be more likely these days to come in contact with this activity in Nepal and India rather than Tibet.

3) *lighting butter lamps/incense* (chö-may/pö pahr): if there are a number of unlit butter lamps near the altar of the monastery you are visiting, you can pay a small price and light one, or as many as you pay for. If not, you can give your money to the person (monk) in charge of the offering and ask that one be lit. You can make a similar offering with incense. The verb used for offering is *phul*, the honorific form of the verb "give". This form shows respect to what or to whom something is offered.

Though donation boxes may be in plain sight, in Tibet there is some concern as to whether or not this money actually remains in the hands of the Tibetans and the monastic community. Be aware as to who is actually receiving the money you are donating.

4) *religious ceremony* (chö-pa phul/shap-den): religious ceremonies are performed for a number of different reasons. Those ceremonies that are regularly performed on the appropriate lunar dates (see DATES AND DAYS OF THE WEEK) differ from special ceremonies called *shap-den*. These are sponsored by private individuals or groups for personal reasons. Rumor has it that westerners have recently sponsored such ceremonies in Tibet.

There is a possibility that you will be in the vicinity of such a ceremony. Sometimes blessed offerings, *tsok*, are passed around. These may be in the form of *tsahm-pa* (roasted barley flour), biscuits, puffed rice, candy, or anything else. Sometimes *tsok* is packaged and handed out, other times you may be offered some from open trays that you can accept with cupped hands—right over left. If sacred water is offered to you, cup your hands in the same way, raise them to your mouth, drink, and continue the motion up to the top of your head, rubbing the moisture into the hair on the sweep back.

5) *religious dance* (chahm): there is great excitement when *chahm* is performed. Traditionally lamas are the dancers and they don masks and colorful costumes for the occasion. Often the dances re-enact actual religious/historical events.

6) *prostration* (cha-tsel): a physical form of religious practice. The practitioner places hands, palms together, at the top of the head, then at the throat, and then at the center of the chest—heart level. These locations symbolize the purification of body, speech, and mind.

Then the practitioner goes down on the knees and touches the forehead on the ground, or in the case of a full-body prostration, stretches the body straight out on the ground, palms together out in front of the head. He or she quickly rises back up and repeats this movement twice more, completing the third round by repeating the hand movements from head to heart while remaining upright.

Some prostrate as often as possible when at sacred places or during certain religious practices. Others prostrate every day throughout their lives, completing numbers in the millions. Sometimes you may see people prostrating themselves around holy places or along circumambulation routes. They stretch out their bodies, step their feet up to where their hands were, and repeat the motion.

7) *bell* (tril-bu): along with the *vajra* (dor-jeh, see –22), the bell is an important religious instrument. The two together (bell and *vajra*) represent the union of all duality, expressed symbolically as the union of male and female attributes. The bell is representative of the female aspect in Tibetan Buddhist philosophy, and symbolizes Wisdom.

8) *bodhisattva* (chang-chup sem-pa): one who forsakes his or her own final release from the cycle of birth and death for the benefit of all sentient beings. Bodhisattvas are born time and again in order to instruct living beings on the teachings of the Buddha. Those who are depicted in statuary and *thang-kas* (religious paintings) are regarded also to be enlightened beings.

9) *mandala* (kyil-khor): a symbol of innate harmony. The most common is a two-dimensional representation of a deity and retinue in the form of a circular composition divided into quadrants with emphasis on the center.

10) *mantra* (ngahk/mah-ni) : a general meaning of *mantra* is a collection of syllables emblematic of a particular deity. The repetition of such is used to call forth the deity, to establish oneself in meditative concentration and to cultivate merit.

Ngahk refers to *mantra* in general. *Mah-ni* is used among Tibetans to denote *mantra* as well, however it technically refers to the ubiquitious *mantra* used by Tibetans: *om mah-ni peh-mey hung*.

11) *mudra* (cha-gyah): hand and body positions both in actual religious practice and in art form. A statue's hand *mudras* provide detailed information as to what is being depicted. There are "teaching *mudras*," "giving *mudras*," and the famous "earth-

witnessing *mudra*'' of the Buddha with alms bowl in his left hand, and right hand touching the ground. With this hand resting on the ground he asks the earth to verify his attainment of immovable silence in the face of countless external disturbances.

12) *nectar* (du-tsi): usually refers to liquid containing a blessing pill, blessing pills themselves, or sacred ointments, all of which are made by lamas. Also as a natural ambrosia, this substance is produced through the process of meditation within the body, as well as in physical places of power. I once saw nectar seep from the roof of a meditation cave upon the conclusion of a practitioner's 1000th round of a particular meditation. Lamas in the area came to verify the substance and called it *du-tsi*.

13) *prayer wheel* (mah-ni kor-lo): these come in various sizes, ranging from small hand-held versions, to ones that tower overhead. They are always spun clockwise so that prayers (*mantras*) located both within and on the external face of the wheel can flow in subtle form away from the wheel to permeate the atmosphere.

14) *protector* (chö-gyal): fierce entities that guard the teachings and practitioners of Tibetan Buddhism, as well as places where the teachings are practiced. You may commonly see these deities at the lower corners of a *thang-ka*, or in the form of statues at monastery entrances.

15) *retinue of a deity* (soong-meh khor): the attendants or followers that surround a deity in iconography serve the same purpose as those that surround a distinguished person.

16) *ritual dagger* (phur-ba): originally brought to Tibet from India (via Nepal), in order to subdue malevolence and remove obstacles. The deity of the dagger is usually depicted looking in all four directions at the top of the knife. You may, on occasion, see these for sale at the bazaar.

17) *rosary* (treng-ah): the Tibetan equivalent has 108 beads, separated into three sections by larger stones, sometimes of different material than the others. At the end, between the 108th and 1st beads, is the *guru* bead. Tibetans usually flip the rosary back upon

itself and continue back the way they came at each complete round. There are counters that hang from the rosary in order to keep track of large numbers of rounds of *mantras* or prostrations (see –6 above), as is required by certain practices.

In addition, certain practices require that the rosary be turned in the left hand and others require that it be turned in the right hand. There are reasons for each. For instance, a reason for holding it in the left hand is said to be because of a nerve that runs from this hand directly to the heart.

18) *scarf* (kah-tah): these come in two fabrics: silk (*ah-shee*) and cotton. They signify the innate purity contained within each living being, and when offered, it is this very purity that is offered. They can be presented to a lama, a lama's throne, statues, and even friends in certain circumstances. If you offer the scarf to a lama, unroll and hold it out to him or her with outstretched arms. He will take the *kah-tah* and probably return it to you by wrapping it around your neck. It is then considered blessed.

19) *stupa* (chor-ten): a reliquary mound constructed using five geometric shapes: the square, symbolizing the element earth; the sphere, symbolizing the element water; the cone is fire; the crescent-like dish is air; and the point, the fifth element in Tibetan Buddhist cosmology, space or ether. *Stupas* are sometimes burial places for famous practitioners and/or their relics; regardless, all *stupas* are considered sacred and thus always passed on a person's right.

20) *teacher and his wife* (rin-po-chay [and] sahng-yum): the title *rinpoche*, literally precious one, is usually used when addressing a *tulku*, a being capable of determining his own future rebirths, who because of his bodhisattva vow (see –8 above), returns countless times in order to benefit sentient beings. If he marries, as is common in some sects, his wife is referred to as his *sahng-yum*, an honorific way to address his spiritual consort.

21) *tutelary deity* (yi-dahm): a deity in male or female form with whom a person has a particular affinity. Though all deities may be respected, it is the *yi-dahm* that one devotes one's practice to.

22) *vajra* (dor-jeh): the male counterpart to the female Wisdom aspect symbolized by the bell (see –7 above). The *vajra* usually symbolizes indestructible Compassion. The two implements are used in precise ways (*mudra*, see –11 above) during religious rituals.

22 Vocabulary List

Words followed by (v) are verbs. Those italicized are in Sanskrit.

a, an:**chik**
a little bit:**de-tsi**
about:**kor-la**
above:**tho-gah la**
accident,to have:**dong-toop** (v)
acquire:**rah** (v)
across:**pha-jo la**
after:**jeh-la**
afternoon:**nying-ku**
again:**yahng-kyer**
age:**lo**
air:**lung**
airplane:**nahm-dru**
airport:**nahm-dru tahng**
all:**tsahng-ma/kahng-gah**
all day:**nying-kahng**
alms:**jim-pa**
alone:**chik-po**
also:**yeh**
although:**yin-neh/yin-nah yahng**
always:**kah-dü yin-nah/tahk-ba-resh**

and:**thang**
angry,to be:**lung lahng** (v)
animal:**sem-chen**
another:**shen-da**
answer:**len gyab** (v)
arm:**lahk-pa**
around here:**di-bah la**
arrive:**lep** (v)
ask:**tri** (v)
aunt (father's sister):**ah-ni**
aunt (mother's sister):**su-mo**
auspicious:**tem-dreh**
avalanche:**kahng-rook**
away:**pha**
baby:**pu-gu**
back:**gyahp**
back (behind):**gyahp-la**
backpack:**gyahp-pah**
bad road:**lahm-kah tsok-pa**
bank:**ngü-khang**
barbershop:**trah-khang**
barley flour:**tsahm-pa**
barter:**jeh** (v)

basin:**toong-pen**

basket:**lo-mah**

bathe:**sug-po tru** (v)

bathroom:**tru-khang**

bead:**treng-dok**

bean:**treh-ma**

bear:**thom**

beard:**gyah**

because:**kah-rey sen-nah**

become:**chhak** (v)

bed:**nye-ti**

beer:**chahng**

before:**ngeh-la**

beggar:**pahng-go**

begin:**go-zoo** (v)

below:**mah**

beside:**thi-la**

between:**pahr-la**

Bhutan:**druk-yool**

bicycle:**kahng-gah-ri**

bird:**chah**

birth:**kye** (v)

birthday:**kye-ba du-chen**

bite:**so gyahp** (v)

black:**nahk-po**

blanket:**nye-jeh**

bleed:**trahk tön** (v)

bloom:**shah** (v)

blow (wind):**lhak-pa gyahp** (v)

blue:**ngom-po**

boat:**dru**

body:**sug-po**

boil:**khö** (v)

book:**teb**/religious:**peh-cha**

border:**sah-tsahm**

borrow:**yahr** (v)

both:**nyi-kah**

bottle:**she-tham**

bottom (deep):**ting**

box:**gahm**

boy:**phu**

bracelet:**dro-toong**

bread:**pah-leh**

break:**chhak** (v)

breakfast:**sho-gey kah-lah**

breathe:**oo gyahp** (v)

bridge:**sahm-pa**

bring:**kye** (v)

broom:**chah-ma**

brown:**gyah-mo**

Buddha:**sahng-gye**

build:**so** (v) / becomes **sö** in
    past tense

build a house:**khang-pa
    gyahp** (v)

bumpy:**bah-ree bu-ree**

burn:**tsi** (v)

but:**yin-neh/yin-nah yahng**

buy:**nyo** (v) / becomes **nyö** in
    past tense

call:**keh tahng** (v)

carry:**kye** (v)

cat:**shi-mee**

catch:**sim** (v)

cave:**trah-pu**

change:**jeh** (v)

cheek:**dem-ba**

chest:**pahng-ko**

chicken:**chah-ti**

child:**pu-gu**

chili:**see-beh**

China:**gyah-nahk**

Christ and Christian:**yi-shu**

churn:**dong-mo**

churn (make tea):**cha so** (v)
cigarette:**tha-ma**
circumambulate:
      ko-rah gyahp (v)
city:**gya-sah**
clear:**sel-po**
climb:**zah** (v)
clock:**chu-tsö**
close:**gyahp** (v)
close door:**go gyahp** (v)
clothes:**thoog-lo**
cloud:**trin-ba**
coat:**chu-ba**
coin,money:**gor-mo** (Chinese
    yuan=**quai**)
college:**lahp-tha**
color:**tsö-shi**
come:**yong/phe** —honorific (v)
cook:**mah-chen**
corn:**ah-shom**
corner:**soor**
corpse:**ro**
cost:**kong**
cough:**lo gyahp** (v)
count:**trahng-kah gyahp** (v)
country:**loong-ba**
cover:**kahp-cho**
cover:**kahp-cho gyahp** (v)
cow:**pah-chu**
crazy:**nyom-pa**
cream:**tri-mah**
crevice:**ser-kah**
crow:**kah-tah**
cup:**pho-ba**
cup(porcelain):**kah-yul**
cure:**trahk** (v)
daily:**nying-tahr**

Dalai Lama:**Yeh-shi Nor-bu**
dance:**shahp-ro gyahp** (v)
date:**tse-ba**
date (western):**in-jee tse-ba**
daughter:**phu-mo**
dawn:**nahm-lahng**
day:**nyi-ma**
day after tomorrow:**nahng-nyi**
day before yesterday:**keh-nyi-ma**
decay:**rool** (v)
deer:**shah-wa**
depth:**ting**
descend:**mah pahp**
desert:**che-thang**
dialect:**keh-luk**
diarrhoea,to have:**tro-go sheh**(v)
dice:**sho**
dictionary:**tah-yeek**
die:**shi** (v)
dinner:**gon-tah kah-lah**
direction:**chok**
directly:**kah-too la**
dirt:**tsok-pa**
disease:**nah-tsa**
ditch:**sah-tong**
dizzy,to be:**go-yoo khor** (v)
do:**che** (v)
doctor:**ahm-jee**
dog:**kyi**
donkey:**phoong-gu**
door:**go**
dough:**tro-ship/pahk**
down:**mah**
dream:**nyi-lahm**
dream:**nyi-lahm tahng** (v)
drink:**thung** (v)
drive:**mo-tah tahng** (v)

drop:**shor** (v)

drunk, to be:**rahp-see** (v)

during:**kahp**

during that time:**deh-thu**

dust:**teh-la**

early:**ngah-bo**

earth:**sah**

east:**shahr**

eat:**sah** (v)

egg:**go-ngah**

electricity:**lohk**

embroidery:**phar-chin**

enter:**zoo** (v)

envelope:**yi-go**

european (foreigner):**chi-gyeh**

evening:**gon-tah**

every/each one:**ray-ray**

everywhere:**kah-sah kah-lah**

exactly:**tahk-tah**

extra:**tho-ba**

eye:**mik**

face:**dong-ba**

factory:**so-tah**

faith:**te-pah**

fall (objects):**sah** (v)

fall (people):**ree** (v)

family:**kim-tsang**

family members:**nahng-mi**

fast:**gyok-po**

fat:**shah gyahk-pa**

father:**pah-la**

fear:**sheh** (v)

festival:**du-chen**

few:**kah-shey**

field:**shing-kah**

fill:**khang** (v)

find:**nye** (v)

finger:**zoo-gu**

finish:**tsahr** (v)

fire:**may**

fireplace:**may-tahng sah**

fish:**nyah**

fix:**so** (v)

flat:**lep lep**

floor:**sah**

flour:**tro-ship**

flower:**meh-toh**

follow:**shoog-la sho** (v)

food:**kah-lah**

foot:**kahng-ba**

forest:**shing-nahk**

forget:**jeh** (v)

fort:**zong**

friend (female):**drok-mo**

friend (male):**drok-po**

friend (helper):**rok-pa**

from:**neh**

from everywhere:**kah-sah kah-neh**

from where:**kah-neh**

fruit:**shing-do**

fry:**ngö** (v)

generally:**mahng-che/man-che-wa**

get:**rah** (v)

get up:**lahng** (v)

get well:**trahk** (v)

girl:**phu-mo**

give:**teh/phul**—honorific (v)

glass:**sheh-go**

go:**dro/phe**—honorific (v)

go down:**mah pahp** (v)

go up:**zah** (v)

goat:**rah**

gold:**ser**

goodbye:**kah-leh phe/kah-leh shoo**

goodnight:**sim-jah nahng-go**

goods:**cha-la**

gorge:**rong**

grab:**sim** (v)

grain:**dru-rik**

grass:**tsah**

green:**jahng-gu**

grow:**kye** (v)

grow cloudy:**nahm tip** (v)

guitar:**dra-nyen**

gun:**men-dah**

hail:**seh-rah tahng** (v)

hair:**trah**

hand:**lahk-pa**

hard:**trahk-po**

hat:**shah-mo**

head:**go**

hear:**koh** (v)

help:**rok-pa tahng** (v)

here:**dhey**

hermit:**gom-chen**

high:**tho-bo**

hill:**ree**

hit:**shu-pa** (v)

horse:**ta**

hospital:**men-khang**

hot spring:**chu zay**

hotel:**dhön-khang**

hour:**chu-tsö**

houseowner:**khang-dahk**

how:**kahn-dre**

how much:**kah-tsö**

hungry,to be:**tro-go thö** (v)

hurry up:**gyok-po sho**

husband:**kyo-gah**

ice:**khyak-pa**

immediately:**lahm-sahng**

in:**nahng-la**

in front of:**tsah la/dün la** —honorific

India:**gyah-gar**

insect:**bu**

inside:**nahng la**

interpreter:**keh-gyoor**

intestines:**gyoo-mah**

invite (to call):**keh tahng** (v)

jacket:**tu-doong**

jewel:**nor-bu**

jewelry:**loo-gyen**

jump:**chom-ja gyahp** (v)

karma:**leh**

keep an eye on:**chah-kah chey** (v)

kerosene:**sah-num**

key:**di-mi**

kill:**say** (v)

kitchen:**tahp-tsahng**

knife:**thi**

know:**shing** (v)

know a person:**ngo shing** (v)

lake:**tso**

lamp:**shu-mah**

language:**keh**

last:**shoog-la**

late:**chi-po**

lazy;bored:**nyop**

lead:**tree** (v)

leak:**tza** (v)

leather:**ko-wa**

ledge:**leh**

left:**yön-ba**

leg:**kahng-ba**

letter:**yi-gi**
library:**pen-zö khang**
life:**tse**
lift:**kyah** (v)
light:**shu-mah**
lightning:**lohk**
like (similar):**nang-shin**
like:**gah** (v)
liver:**chin-ba**
lock:**gon-jah**
long:**ring-bo**
long distance:**tha ring-bo**
long time:**thu-tsö ring-bo**
look:**tah** (v)
loose:**lhook lhook**
loosen:**loo-roo tahng** (v)
lose:**lah** (v)
lose (game):**shor** (v)
low:**mah-bo**
lunch:**nying-ku kah-lah**
mah jong:**bah**
make:**so** (v)
many:**mahng-bo**
map:**sahp-tah**
market:**trom**
match:**tsahk-tra**
mattress:**bö-den**
maybe:**chik che-nah**
meander:**chahm chahm la dro** (v)
measure:**tsay gyahp** (v)
meat:**shah**
medicine:**men**
meditate:**gom gyahp** (v)
meet:**toop** (v)
message:**len**
middle:**kyi-la**
milk:**o-mah**

minute:**kar-mah**
mirror:**she-go**
mistake:**nor** (v)
monastery:**gom-pa**
money:**ngü**
Mongolia:**sog-po**
monk:**trah-pa;ku-sho**
monk's robe:**zen**
monkey:**pi-yu** (said quickly like
    piu)
month:**dah-wah**
moon:**dah-wah**
morning:**sho-gey**
mother:**ah-mah**
mountain:**ree**
mountain pass:**lah**
mountain (snow):**kahng-ree**
mouse:**tsee tsee**
mouth:**kha**
move:**pö** (v)
movie (show):**teh-mo**
mud:**tahk-pa**
Muslim:**kah-chi**
mutton:**luk-shah**
naga (snake god):**loo**
name:**ming/tsen**—honorific
near:**nye-bo**
need:**goh** (v)
needle:**kahp**
neighbor:**kyim-tse**
Nepal:**peh-yool**
never:**kah-dü-yeh** (+ negative
    verb)
night:**tsen**
nomad:**drog-pa**
noodle:**gyah thook**
noon:**nying-ku**

north:**chahng**
northeast:**chahng-shar**
northwest:**chahng-noop**
nose:**nah-gu**
now:**than-dah/tha**
nowadays:**thi-ring-sahng**
nowhere:**kah-bah-yeh min-du**
number:**trahng-kah**
nunnery:**ah-ni gom-pa**
ocean:**gyah-tso**
office:**leh-khung**
oil:**num**
ointment:**chook-pa**
okay:**di-gi-ray**
on:**gahng la**
on either side:**yeh-yön**
onion:**tsöng**
opposite/the other side:
        pha-chok
orange (color):**li-wahng**
orange (fruit):**tsha-lu-mah**
other:**shen-dah**
otherwise:**yah-meh-nah**
outside:**chi-lo lah**
overflow:**lu** (v)
pain:**sook**
paint:**tsön**
paint:**tsön tahng** (v)
painting:**ri-mo**
pan:**hai-yahng**
pants:**khu-doong**
paper:**shu-gu**
parents:**pha-mah**
passport (all permits):**lah-kyer**
path:**kahng-lahm**
pay:**ngü teh** (v)
peach:**kahm-bu**

peak:**tse**
peel:**pahk-pa shu** (v)
pen:**nyu-gu**
pencil:**shah-nyu**
person/people:**mi**
photograph:**pahr**
photograph:**pahr gyahp** (v)
picnic:**ling-ka**
picnic:**ling-ka tahng** (v)
pig:**pahk-pa**
pill:**ri-pu**
pillow:**nye-goh**
place:**sah-cha**
place of pilgrimage:**neh-sah/
        neh-kor sah**
place of retreat:**tsham-khang**
plate:**tha-ba**
play cards:**sho-bahk tshe** (v)
pleasant:**kyi-bo**
pork:**pahk-shah**
post office:**drah-khang**
potato:**sho-go**
pour:**lu** (v)
powder:**che-ma/ship-ship**
practise/learn:**jahng** (v)
pray:**mu-lahm gyahp** (v)
prayer flag:**thar-cho**
press:**tsir** (v)
price:**kong**
price,drop:**kong chahk** (v)
price,raise:**kong phar** (v)
probably:**yin-ba-drah**
probably not:**meh-ba-drah**
profit:**khep-sahng**
prostrate:**cha-tsel** (v)
province:**zong-wa**
purple:**gyah-moo**

pus:**nahk**
put:**shah** (v)
question:**tri** (v)
quilt:**phö-kheb**
rabbit:**ri-pong**
rain:**char-pa**
rain:**char-pa tahng** (v)
rainbow:**jah**
razor:**trah-tri**
reach (with hand):**nyop** (v)
read:**lo** (v)
record (tape):**keh-pahr so** (v)
red:**mahr-po**
religious ceremony:
  chö-pah phul/shap-den
religious dance:**chahm**
religious painting:**thang-ka**
religious scarf:**kah-tah**
remember:**theng** (v)
rent:**khang-la**
repair:**so kyor** (v)
rest:**ngal-su gyahp** (v)
restaurant:**sah-khang**
return (from away):
  loh yong (v)
rib:**tsee-mah**
rice:**dre**
rich:**chook-po**
ride (horse):**ta shön** (v)
right:**yeh-ba**
ring:**tsi-ko**
rinse:**sheh tahng** (v)
ripe:**mim-pa**
rise:**lahng** (v)
river:**tsahng-po**
road:**lahm-kah**
rob:**ku-ma kool** (v)

rock:**doh**
roof:**tho-gah**
rope:**tahg-pa**
rot:**rool** (v)
rotten:**roo-ba**
rough:**tsu-po**
rub:**phu phu tahng** (v)
run:**gyuk-sha loh** (v)
Russia:**oo-roo-su**
rust:**tsha**
salt:**tsha**
sand:**che-mah**
say:**lahp** (v)
scarf:**kah-ti**
school:**lahp-tha**
scold:**shey shey tahng** (v)
scripture:**peh-chah**
season:**nahm-tu**
see:**thong** (v)
sell:**tsong** (v)
send:**tahng** (v)
sentence:**tsik-drup**
servant:**yok-po**
sew:**tsem-bu gyahp** (v)
sharpen:**dar** (v)
sheep:**luk**
shirt:**wahn-joo**
shoe:**lahm**
short cut:**gyok-lahm**
short distance:**tha nye-bo**
shout:**keh gyahp** (v)
show:**teh** (v)
shrine:**lha-khang**
sick,to be:**nah** (v)
side:**chok**
sign:**tahk**
Sikkim:**den-jong**

silver:**ngü**
sing:**shey tahng** (v)
sister (older):**ah-cha**
sister (younger):**noo-mo**
sit:**deh/shoo**—honorific (v)
situation:**neh-tahng**
size:**che-choong**
skin:**pahk-pa**
sky:**nahm**
sleep:**nyi-ku** (v)
sleeve:**phu-doong**
slow:**kah-leh**
smoke:**tu-wa**
snake:**drul**
snow:**kahng**
snow:**kahng pahp** (v)
snow mountain:**kahng-ree**
soap:**yi-tsi**
sock:**oh-mu-soo**
soft:**jahm-bo**
sometimes:**tsahm tsahm/
      kahp kahp**
song:**shey**
soon:**gyok-po**
sore:**mah**
soup:**thook-pa**
south:**lo**
southeast:**shar lo**
southwest:**noop lo**
spice:**meh-nah**
spoon:**thu-mah**
sprain:**tseek tro** (v)
spring:**gyu-chu**
stairs:**ken-zah**
stand:**lahng** (v)
star:**kar-mah**
start:**go zoo** (v)

stomach:**tro-go**
stop:**kahk** (v)
store:**tsong-khang**
storm:**loong-tsup**
stove:**thap**
straight:**sha-gya**
strange:**ken-tsa-bo**
street:**lahm-kah**
string:**ku-pa**
student:**lahp-tha-wa** (or)
      lop-trook
stupa:**chor-ten**
sugar:**che-ma ka-ra**
sun:**nyi-ma**
sunny,to be:**nyi-ma shah** (v)
swallow:**mi-gyu** (v)
sweep:**khay-gyahp** (v)
table:**chog-tse**
tailor:**tsem-so**
take:**len** (v)
take (lead):**tree** (v)
take away:**kye** (v)
talk:**keh-cha shey** (v)
tavern:**chahng-khang**
tea:**cha**
tea (sweet):**cha ngar-mo**
tea (Tibetan):**Phö cha**
teach:**lahp** (v)
teacher:**geh-gen**
tear:**rey** (v)
telephone:**kha-bahr**
telephone:**kha-bahr tahng** (v)
temperature:**tsah-wa**
tent:**koor**
that:**pha-gi**
there:**pha-ghey**
these:**din-tso**

these days:**thi-ring-sahng**

thigh:**lah-shah**

thing:**cha-la**

thirsty,to be:**kha-kom** (v)

this:**di**

throat:**mik-pa**

throw:**yoo** (v)

thunder:**dru-keh** (literally "dragon's voice")

thunder:**dru-keh gyahp** (v)

Tibet:**Phö**

tie:**dahm** (v)

tiger:**tahk**

tigress:**tah-mo**

time:**thu-tsö**

tired,to be:**thang che** (v)

today:**thi-ring**

toilet:**sahng-chö**

tomorrow:**sahng-nyi**

tongue:**chay**

tonight:**to-gong**

tool:**lahk-cha**

tooth:**so**

tooth brush:**so-tru**

touch:**lahk-pa chang** (v)

towel:**ah-cho**

town:**trong-sehp**

train:**ri-li**

tree:**shing dong**

try:**thup-shi che** (v)

turn:**kor** (v)

umbrella:**nyi-du**

uncle:**ah-ku**

under:**woh-la**

understand:**ha-kho** (v)

up:**yah**

upstairs:**tho-gah**

urine:**chin-pa**

useful,to be:**phen-thok** (v)

valley:**loong-shon/rong**

vegetable:**tshey**

very:**shi-tah**

village:**trong-sehp**

visa (all permits):**lah-kyer**

vomit:**gyuk-pa kyu** (v)

wait:**gu** (v)

wake:**lahng** (v)

walk:**khom-ba gyahp** (v)

wall:**tsik-pa**

warm:**tro-po**

wash:**tru** (v)

waste:**tor** (v)

water:**chu**

waterfall:**pahp-chu**

weather:**nahm-shi**

week:**dün-tha**

weigh:**kyah** (v)

west:**noop**

what:**kah-rey**

whatever:**kah-rey yin-neh**

wheat:**tro**

wheel:**kor-lo**

when:**kah-dü**

whenever:**kah-dü yin-neh**

where:**kah-bah**

wherever:**kah-bah yin-neh**

whiskey:**ah-rah**

white:**kahr-po**

why:**kah-rey che-neh**

wife:**kyi-men**

win:**thop** (v)

wind:**lung;lahk-pa**

window:**gi-khung**

wipe:**chi** (v)

woman:**kyi-men**
wood:**shing**
word:**tsik**
world:**zahm-bu-ling**

write:**thi** (v)
year:**lo**
yellow:**ser-po**
yesterday:**keh-sah**